Dufay to Sweelinck

Netherlands Masters of Music

Dufay to Sweelinck

Netherlands Masters of Music

By EDNA RICHOLSON SOLLITT

Author of
Mengelberg and the Symphonic Epoch

GREENWOOD PRESS, PUBLISHERS
WESTPORT, CONNECTICUT

The Library of Congress cataloged this book as follows:

Sollitt, Edna Richolson.
    Dufay to Sweelinck: Netherlands masters of music.
Westport, Conn., Greenwood Press ₁1970₁

    163 p. 23 cm.

    Reprint of the 1933 ed.

    1. Composers, Dutch. 2. Music—Netherlands—History and criti-
cism.   I. Title.

ML390.S66   1970   780'.922 [B]   79-100843
ISBN 0-8371-4028-5   MARC

Library of Congress   71 ₁4₁   MN

Originally published in 1933 by Ives Washburn, New York

Reprinted from an original copy in the collections of the
Brooklyn Public Library

Reprinted by Greenwood Press,
a division of Williamhouse-Regency Inc.

First Greenwood reprinting 1970
Second Greenwood reprinting 1976

Library of Congress Catalog Card Number 79-100843

ISBN 0-8371-4028-5

Printed in the United States of America

To
WILLEM MENGELBERG

1

CONTENTS

FOREWORD

DURING THE FIFTEENTH and sixteenth centuries,
Netherlands musicians were active and influential throughout Europe; this is usually
designated in musical history as the "Netherlands period."

It is a period which lies within clearly
defined limits; and from its beginning at the
maturity of Dufay to its close at the death of
Sweelinck it presents an unbroken continuity
of artistic achievement: for these reasons it
invites to unity of consideration. The present
book is, notwithstanding, the first work to
accord it this unity.

The structural plan of the work provides,
also for the first time, a guidance for following
the development and the course of influence
of Netherlands art; this guidance has hitherto
been entirely lacking; and only at the end of
long research and effort came the ordered

sequence and grouping which form the outline of this book. Once achieved, this outline has an appearance of simple inevitability very deceiving to the casual eye.

Attention may well be drawn here to the important fact that, in several chapters, there is presented a great deal of valuable and interesting material which has not before been available to the musician or the general reader, for the reason that the study of this material necessitated recourse to many sources, widely scattered, not often accessible without special privilege, and requiring familiarity with Latin, old Flemish, and modern Dutch, in addition to French, German, and Italian.

The direct access to authentic sources has made possible meticulous accuracy not to be attained by study restricted to derivative material.

Although I have already expressed my thanks to them individually, I add here also the most grateful acknowledgment of the help I have received with the work from those

FOREWORD

who placed at my disposal the treasures of libraries and collections in several countries, aided me with their distinguished prestige and their own rare erudition, and — not least — encouraged me in a task which has been as arduous as it was full of joy.

Amsterdam,
June, 1932

I

THE FIRST NETHERLANDS SCHOOL

THIS NAME, the "First Netherlands School," is a convenient designation for a group of eminent composers of the fifteenth century. It is a term at once too arbitrary and too lax, but it has the sanction of centuries of tolerant acceptance, for it is not easy otherwise to group these composers. To assign them here by date is to ignore the fact that, in this respect, Busnois almost parallels Okeghem; to make artistic methods the test is to be brought to a pause before some of the works of Dufay, Busnois, and Faugues. Convenience alone can excuse the use of the classification.

[13]

To this School belong three very great names: Dufay, Binchois, and Busnois. All three were under the patronage of the house of Burgundy. Among the art-loving dynasties of Renaissance Europe none deserves a more grateful attention from the musical historian. Six generations of this princely house exerted a powerful influence upon musical development, an influence extending well-nigh throughout the two centuries of Netherlands' glory. From Philippe the Good to Philippe II of Spain, the Burgundian sovereigns gave to music a patronage as remarkable for enlightened judgment and cultivated taste as for regal generosity.

Of Philippe the Good, in whose service both Dufay and Binchois flourished, Van der Straeten gives us an interesting glimpse. "This prince did not wish to be surpassed by any sovereign in Christendom in the generous patronage of music. He attached to his service the most renowned artists, in a way to merit the eulogy of a contemporary writer, who says that his chapel 'is one of the best and most melodious to be found anywhere.' Philippe engaged expert miniaturists to illuminate and calligraph the musical works which he loved best, especially those compositions which were used in the perpetual Masses which he endowed for the benefit of the Order of the Golden Fleece. The Duke was known also as an excellent dancer; as the choreographic art was rigorously submitted to rhythmic and musical laws, we may conclude that Philippe understood something of those laws."

Charles the Bold was the patron of Busnois, and himself a musician deserving of our appreciation. He loved music not only as a luxury favored by princes, but also for the extreme pleasure which he truly derived from hearing the virtuosi in his employ His private chapel was the object of his most assiduous care. Every day his choirs sang there, and the music was chosen from the Duke's wide selection of the world's best. The choirs were accompanied by a notable orchestra. The musicians of the chapel included twenty-four singers, a boy-choir, an organist, lutist, and players of viols and oboes. Mass was performed for Charles every day; indeed, it was the event of the day, a great musical enjoyment as well as a religious ceremony. So deep was the love of Charles for music, that he caused many of the singers and the players, with their instruments, to be carried with him when he went to the siege of Neuss.

The musical talent of Charles the Bold has been celebrated by a number of historians, including Olivier de la Marche, who calls the Burgundian prince an innate artist, excellently trained As a youth at the court of his father, Philippe the Good, Charles had requested lessons from Robert Morton, a singer in the ducal chapel. When he had his own court, Charles continued his studies with Busnois. He prized highly the services of this musician, and many documents record his benefactions to Busnois.

The ability and skill of Charles are proved by an incident recorded in the local archives at Cambrai; it is there stated that when Charles the Bold was in that city in 1460 he composed a motet which was sung by the choirs of the Cathedral. The Duke was himself able to sing, and was gifted with a clear and sonorous voice. Among instruments he preferred the harp; from the tenderest age he loved to play upon it, using a small instrument from one of the best Netherlands makers.

Busnois was the finest ornament of Charles' chapel; upon the accession of the Duke's daughter, Mary of Burgundy, the musician retained his position and the affectionate appreciation of the court. While Mary did not inherit such a passion for music as had animated Charles, she at least "cultivated the art with taste." She was taught in childhood by a distinguished Netherlander, Pierre Beurse, and was an excellent performer upon the clavichord. Her romantic union with Maximilian, prince, poet, and artist, was of the happiest; Maximilian lived at Utrecht following strenuous wars against the French, and the palace there was also never without virtuosi.

We shall follow further the musical story of the house of Burgundy in chapters which deal with the musicians loved and honored by Philippe the Fair, Margaret of Austria, and the noble Charles V. Let us now consider the known details concerning the composers of the First Netherlands School.

GUILLAUME DUFAY

A DISTINGUISHED POSITION IN ART was accorded to Dufay by the early theorists and musical historians; Adam von Fulda mentions him with highest praise, as do Gafor, Seybald Heyden, and Hermann Finck; Tinctoris speaks of him in superlative terms in the "Ars contrapuncti." This homage was strangely followed by a complete ignoring of Dufay by the eighteenth-century historians, Hawkins and Burney; and their contemporary, Forkel, stated erroneously that no single note of his work had survived. Later, through the labors of Kiesewetter and Haberl, we were put into possession of a large number of Dufay's works.

Little is known concerning his life. Early writers give a few facts; after this nothing is added except conjecture. The most exact and dependable summaries concerning Dufay's life we owe to Eitner and Van den Borren.

Dufay was born in Hainault about 1400. According to Eitner, he was in boyhood a chorister at the Cathedral of Cambrai. From December, 1428, he was enrolled as a singer in the Papal Chapel. In 1437 Dufay began his period of service with Philippe the Good, Duke of Burgundy. It would appear that he must previously have taken Holy Orders, since he was given the canonicat of Cambrai on March 21, 1437. It is believed that he was in Paris at the time of entering the priesthood. Dufay spent seven years in Savoy, but no documents give us the dates for the period. He passed the closing years of his life at Cambrai, where he died on November 27, 1474.

Among the works of Dufay which we possess are numerous Masses, motets, and songs to French texts. They are in the Papal Archives at Rome, and in libraries at Paris, Brussels, Cambrai, Vienna, Trieste, Bologna, and Modena.

ÉGIDE BINCHOIS

THE MOST FAMOUS CONTEMPORARY of Dufay was Binchois, so called from his birthplace, Binche, near Mons in Hainault. In his youth he was a soldier; a lament was written on his death, beginning thus:

> En sa jeunesse il fut soudart
> d'honorable mondanité,
> puis a eslu la meilleur part
> servant Dieu en humilité.

In 1437 Binchois was Maître de chapelle to the Duke of Burgundy, and "received 24 lire 'for a book which he had made and composed of Passions in a new manner'"'; this notation appears again in 1452. Documents in the city archives of Brussels show that he was appointed Prebendary of the Church of St. Woudru at Mons in 1438; in 1452 he received the office of second chapelain to Philippe. In the records of the ducal Chapel for 1465 Binchois is not mentioned, and this is the date generally accepted as that of his death; Van der Straeten assigns 1460.

Binchois was honored for his personal character (in the Lament he is called "patron de bonté"), and his art has been greatly admired. Hermann Finck, in 1556, classes him with Dufay and Busnois, and calls him one of the musicians who have benefited the art by his discoveries and study. Tinctoris praises him as "a composer who has made an immortal name for himself by his admirable compositions." His fame reached as far as Italy, although it appears that he never went there. Gafor considers Binchois an authority.

Brussels possesses a three-voice Mass by

Binchois; in the Vatican Library are secular songs and motets, with the manuscript of his best-known song, "Ce mois de May"; there are extant also several fragments of Masses. Riemann in 1892 and Stainer in 1898 published a number of chansons in modern notation. Riemann, in studying the notation of Binchois for this edition, concluded that he was older than Dufay.

The name is variously given as Binchoy, Binchoys, Buchoi, Winchois, de Binck.

ANTON BUSNOIS

THE THIRD of these most important early Netherlanders was Busnois. No record has yet been found concerning his birth. The first dated documents which we possess are the bills for court personnel of the chapel of Charles the Bold; these are from 1467, and show Busnois as a singer in the chapel. As we have noted, many years were passed by Busnois in the service of the Burgundian court. It was a life of comfort, care-free; and his princely patrons were in heartiest sympathy with artistic effort.

The name of Busnois appears in the bills for court service of Mary of Burgundy as late as October 26, 1480; Eitner states February 2, 1481. Busnois did not, however, die at that time, as was formerly supposed; he passed twelve years as singer at the Church of St. Sauveur at Bruges, where his death is officially recorded on November 6, 1492. This fact we owe to the researches of Van der Straeten.

The early historians give high praise to Busnois; Tinctoris offered a remarkable sign of his distinguished opinion by dedicating to him and Okeghem jointly a work on musical theory. Adam von Fulda speaks of Busnois as "worthiest musician"; Pietro Aron includes him with the best in his art.

We possess numerous compositions of Busnois, and they belong to the most important of his age. The four-voice Mass, "Ecce ancilla," may almost be called the leading work of the period; together with the Mass of like name by Dufay it forms a standard for judging the progress of music in his time. "His is an art," says Ambros, "that is bolder and surer than that of preceding times; the use of counterpoint and canon is fluent, strong, and effective. Busnois can lead voices with the simplest clarity as well as in complex and syncopated combinations."

Of Busnois' works there are extant seven songs published in the Petrucci "Canti cento-cinquanta" (1503); a few motets and Masses in Brussels and Rome; a manuscript at Dijon; and at Florence fourteen songs, "of an originality, finish, and elegance which prove Busnois a master of secular song," according to Ambros. The most famous of these are the Christmas song, "Noë, Noë," and the "Dieu quel mariage." The songs of Busnois were frequently used as themes by later composers.

HEYNE (*Heinrich van Ghizegem*)

A CONTEMPORARY of Busnois was Heinrich van Ghizegem, called Heyne, Hayne, or Ayne, a Netherlander also in the service of the chapel of Charles the Bold of Burgundy. He appears in the bills as "chantre de chambre." One of his songs, in the Dijon Codex, is unusual for the time, in that the voices do not cross each other. Other works of this composer are in the British Museum, and published in Petrucci collections and in the Odhecaton. Like those of Busnois, Heyne's songs were much loved and used.

JACQUES BARBIREAU

BARBIREAU is another composer of that period; we have a few facts concerning his life, and some of his work has come down to us. Eitner calls him "of Hainault." From 1448 he was choirmaster at Notre Dame, Antwerp, holding this position until his death on August 8, 1491. In this placement he was the predecessor of Obrecht. Among his known compositions are Masses in four and in five parts, a Kyrie, and some songs; most of these are in the Imperial Library of Vienna. The name is given also as Barbingaut, Barbiryanus, and Barbacola.

VINCENT FAUGUES

WE MUST NOW CONSIDER those whose lives are totally unknown to us, but whose works have happily survived their personal oblivion and are of a quality to command attention. Among these the foremost are Faugues and Caron. The works of Faugues are in the Papal Chapel; they appeared in the time of Pope Nicolas V, between 1447 and 1455, and include a three-voice Mass, "Omme armé," and two other Masses. The voice-leading is skilful, and he has a melodic gift. "In all the work of Faugues there is something gentler, tenderer, weaker — if you will — than Dufay; and against the strong, masculine expression of later composers he is a great contrast," writes Ambros.

In the Kyrie of the Mass "Omme armé" occurs a significant use of the theme in repetition a fifth above, followed by its appearance

again on the original tone; this shows Faugues
striving for a musically interesting and logical
structure. This fugal device, his syncopation
in certain examples, and his use of cantus
firmus adroitly surrounded by contrapuntal
figuration make him noteworthy.

CARON (*Firmin or Philippe*)

ANOTHER OF this group is Caron, Latinized
Carontis, "worthy of a place beside Busnois."
Tinctoris has used his song, "La Tridaine,"
as an example in his work on counterpoint.
Several of Caron's works are in the Papal
archives; these include a Mass which shows
interesting analogies with the work of Dufay
and Faugues. "His extant compositions show
unity, a fullness of harmony, a strength and
consistency not met before," says Ambros.

"What existence more obscure than that
of Caron, a distinguished composer of the
fifteenth century, who shared with Busnois,
Obrecht, Okeghem, and others the glory of
contributing to the progress of music in the

Netherlands!" So writes Van der Straeten. It is not certain where Caron was born; authorities disagree concerning his name, which is given by Haberl and Eitner as Philippe, and as Firmin by Van der Straeten, following Tinctoris.

The only works of Caron which have come down to us are a few Masses in the Papal Chapel, a group of secular songs in the Dijon Codex, and manuscripts at Paris and Cambrai.

PHILIPPE BASIRON (*Bassiron*)

BASIRON was a Netherlands composer of the fifteenth century. No details of his life are known to us. Masses and motets are in Petrucci collections, and manuscripts in the Papal Archives and the Imperial Library of Vienna.

ELOY (?)

ELOY, considered a contemporary of Faugues, was called by Tinctoris "a composer highly skilful in the use of modes." His great Mass, "Dixerunt discipuli," in the Papal Archives, gives an excellent specimen of his work. "In his art he attains an elevation of style more notable than is encountered in the work of any other member of the First Netherlands School," declares Ambros. Gafor mentions Eloy as most learned. Fétis draws attention to the fact that there are still families of this name in Hainault and Flanders.

JOHANNES REGIS is known to us by works of merit preserved in Petrucci collections; Tinctoris praises his skill. Jean Brassart must also be mentioned among the Netherlanders of the "First School."

II

JEAN OKEGHEM

Okeghem is one of the important figures in musical history. His own work was a great artistic achievement, comprehending and surpassing the progress of his predecessors; and his influence as teacher and example was of such value that he has frequently been called "the source and father of all music since his time."

We are in possession of a rich heritage of his compositions, and have accurate documentary material regarding the greater part of his life. Much of the biographical data has been available only in recent times; the efforts of Burbure and Van der Straeten left incomplete a wide space which Brenet, working in France, was able to fill only as lately as 1893. With somewhat heavy strokes Brenet demolishes the conjectures regarding Okeghem's middle life, substituting documents for speculation. Okeghem is now the first and one of the few among the Netherlands composers concerning whom it is possible to write an almost complete life-sketch, with every fact supported by authentic records.

A family named Okeghem appears in the city records of Termonde, East Flanders, in the fourteenth century. The name is a rare one, and it is probable that the composer came from this family. The year of his birth is not yet known, but is tentatively placed at 1430.

In the "Ars contrapuncti" of Tinctoris, written in 1476, it is stated that Okeghem was a pupil of Dufay, was "glorified in having had Dufay for a master." With this clear statement from a careful contemporary before us, it is strange to find nineteenth-century writers tilting over the question, and Brenet omitting all mention of Dufay.

In the records of Antwerp Cathedral is a document mentioning Okeghem as a singer there during the year from June, 1443 to 1444. The year 1446 brings us a tailor's bill proving that Okeghem was in the chapel of Charles of Bourbon; and a record of 1452–3 places him at the head of the non-priestly singers of the chapel of Charles VII of France. Precious documents from 1454 to 1459 mention him, "with the name always mangled by the scribes," Brenet says, as receiving payments for special services; in 1461 he is given mourning attire for the funeral of his patron Charles. Brenet states that "Charles had, a few years before his death, rewarded the services of his zealous and talented chapelain by the gift of one of the highest dignities at his disposition in the kingdom: that of Treasurer of the Abbey of St. Martin at Tours." The date of this appointment lies between 1456 and 1459.

This dignity was accompanied by numerous

privileges which made it one of the most lucrative offices of the churches of France. Okeghem was even dispensed from the necessity of residence there. Altogether, it would be impossible to imagine the musician more comfortably situated. Bills for the following years show the payment of his gages and many special allowances. Okeghem kept the functions and dignities, and also the emoluments of this office through the reign of Louis XI, and the accession of Charles VIII made no change in his status.

The ceremonies in which the Treasurer took part surpassed in magnificence even those of the Roman basilicas, according to the testimony of an Italian writer, Francesco Florio. For special occasions this pomp was doubled. From statements in the records we find that the Treasurer's duties were as follows: to guard the sepulchre of St. Martin and his relics; and to have custody of the treasure, for which he held the keys. In the treasury were kept not only the rich objects and ornaments of one of the most heavily endowed churches in Christendom, but also the charters concerning the kingdom of France, placed at St. Martin's by the piety of the King.

Certain authorities mention a voyage of Okeghem to Spain in 1469, but their basis for this is not known; Brenet does not mention it, though she states that documents from Tours contain almost yearly records of Okeghem from 1459 to 1494.

In the archives of St. Donatus in Bruges, Van der Straeten found a most interesting document relating to the visit of Okeghem to that city in 1484. Okeghem arrived in Bruges on August 15th of that year; he was at that time first chapelain of the French king. The excerpt reads: "Sex cannae vini, pro subsidio sociorum de musica in coena facta domino thesaurio Turonensi, domino Johanni Okeghem, primo capellano regis Franciae, musico excellentissimo, cum suis."

This journey was made at the king's expense, but it is clear that the Netherlands city

added its share to the festivities; and
Okeghem's pupils and colleagues at Bruges
entertained him with great honors, which cul-
minated, we read, in a magnificent banquet.
Anyone familiar with Netherlands hospital-
ity in our own comparatively restrained time
may well believe that the mediaeval reception
of so great a countryman was worthy of the
word magnificent. There is probably no other
place in the world where an eminent musician
is welcomed as he is welcomed in the Netherlands; this is true today, and it was evidently
true four hundred and fifty years ago.

Okeghem remained at Tours to the end of
his life, "honored by nobles and people."
There is an entry in the Abbey records concerning his replacement; this is dated February 9, 1496; as Okeghem is mentioned frequently until 1494, and then disappears from
the records, his death is presumptively between 1494–1496. There has been found as yet
no document concerning it.

There are three famous "déplorations,"

laments, upon the death of Okeghem; those of Guillaume Crétin and Josquin Deprès are famous, while that of Erasmus is less known. The Crétin "Déploration" consists of more than four hundred verses in French; it is filled with eulogy of Okeghem's art and of his personal virtues. In it Crétin addresses the predecessors, contemporaries, and successors of Okeghem, and this is useful in fixing dates previous to which certain musicians died, because these are mentioned by Crétin among the deceased. The work opens thus:

> Par quarante ans et plus il a servy
> Sans quelque ennuy en sa charge et office
> De trois Roys a tant l'amour desservy, etc.

Here is mention of Okeghem's more than forty years of continuous service, under Charles VII, Louis XI, and Charles VIII, a career entirely pursued in France; this is in strong contrast with the careers of many other musicians who, through necessity or "a roving humor," passed from the Papal Chapel to the service of one distant sovereign after another, sometimes settling late in life in some city of the homeland where benefices awaited them. The quiet existence of Okeghem at St. Martin's did not, however, prevent his fame from spreading far and wide, even early in his life. Another Lament, that of Josquin, follows in its entirety; it is given here as it appears in Kiesewetter's "Verdienste der Niederländer um die Tonkunst:"

> Nymphes des bois, Déesses de fontaines,
> Chantres experts de toutes nations!
> Changez vos voix fort claires et hautaines
> En cris tranchantz et lamentations:
> Car d'Atropos les molestations
> Votre Okeghem par la rigeur attrappe,
> Le vray trésoir de Musique et chef-d'oeuvre.
> Qui de Tropos désormais plus n'échappe?
> Dont grant doumage est que la terre le couvre.
> Accoustrez vous d'habitz de deuil,
> Jusquin, Brumel, Pierchon, Compère!

The text of this Lament follows a cantus firmus from the Church Requiem Mass. Ambros says that "it towers above other Lamentations like a proud and grave cypress."

DUFAY TO SWEELINCK

The little-known Lament of Erasmus is about seventy lines in length, and begins as follows:

> Joanni Okego, musico summo
> Ergo ne conticuit
> Vox illa quondam nobilis,
> Aurea vox Okegi?
> Sic musicae extinctum decus?

Besides these posthumous celebrations of the art and virtues of Okeghem, there had previously been composed in his honor a piece by Busnois, with Latin text, set for four voices; and Tinctoris had dedicated to Okeghem and Busnois jointly his "Liber de natura et proprietate tonorum."

The known works of Okeghem consist of about fifty pieces. The most careful and painstaking students of these compositions have not been able to decide upon their chronological order. Among the works are Masses, many of which present great difficulties in notation, the understanding of which, Brenet says, "depends upon a profound acquaintance with ecclesiastical formulae." There are numerous motets and many chansons, including "Baisez-moi, donc," "Dung altre amer," and "Malheur me bat."

We arrive now at the most famous work of Okeghem: the astonishing motet for thirty-six voices. Fétis absolutely refused to believe in the existence of this work, saying that such a composition was quite impossible; in the 15th century, he pointed out, the use of even six voices was rare. The witnesses to the existence of the work were, however, formal and repeated. The first reference is in a passage in the poem of Crétin, at a date so close to Okeghem's death that no writer would place to his credit a work "absolutely impossible"; the very terms in which Crétin writes, on the contrary, prove the admiration which this composition excited in the contemporaries of Okeghem. Then Ornitoparchus mentions it; then Glarean; then Claude Sebastien. According to Ambros, writing previous to 1868, later research would prove it to be no myth.

And now we have had it identified, in a collection which contains also a piece of Josquin's for twenty-four voices. The Okeghem work is noted, as the prescient Ambros stated it would be, for a few voices only, with canons indicated and different themes assigned. It is written for four voices forming upon four themes a canon of nine parts, with text merely "Deo gratias." Strangely Eitner, who knew of this identification, makes no mention of the composition.

The honor in which Okeghem was held by his contemporaries caused the finest talents to come to him as a teacher; among these were Josquin Deprès and Pierre de la Rue; and when we think of the magnificent line of musicians extending from these artists and the other pupils of Okeghem into every country of Europe, we must agree with Ambros that "Okeghem may rightly be called, in all honor, the father and source of all following generations of musicians." This is so sweeping a statement for the careful Ambros to make, that I doubted my first reading, and three times, at long intervals, verified the literal accuracy of my translation!

As Brenet says, anyone writing about Okeghem should conclude with a quotation from Ambros; here follows part of his beautiful tribute to Okeghem; it is one of the many passages from Ambros which make me feel that he well deserves the immortality which he has helped to give to others:

"Okeghem is original and interesting; his intricacies of counterpoint, his canon movements, however strict and skilful, have had breathed into them his singing soul. There are found in his works whole periods, often in the middle voices, of most wonderful melodic leading, and of extraordinary tenderness and intimacy of expression. One example is the song 'Je n'ai deuil.' His harmonies are not merely ancient and strange; they have sound and body.

"That his compositions are not merely tours de force, but were workable and popular, is proved by copies in the archives of the Chapel, copies in which the singers have made notations between the staves, and in which a misprint is carefully corrected.

"A last shining ray on Okeghem's old age is contained in the songs which masters like Josquin and Lupi wrote on his death. We must remember that when, in these poems, Josquin, Gaspar, and the rest call Okeghem their 'master and good father,' it was at a time when they were themselves world-famous artists."

III

JACOB OBRECHT

"**A** GREAT, profound, earnest, and manly artist, whose works, almost without exception, show a character of sublimity, is Jacob Obrecht, born about 1430 in Utrecht. Among the composers before Josquin he is the mightiest phenomenon. The tonal art made a more important development and harmony a greater progress in his work than with Okeghem, with whose method and manner Obrecht's art shares all the finesse, subtlety, and skill, all the understanding of tonal structure. His glory may well vie with that of Okeghem." Thus does Ambros begin his study of Obrecht, one of the proudest names which Netherlands art history can boast.

The works of Obrecht have come down to us with almost unexampled completeness. His life is not known with such fullness; there are, however, sufficient records in our possession to form the basis for a biography which is authentic if somewhat scanty.

Obrecht's birth at Utrecht about 1430 is accepted by Eitner, Van der Straeten, Ambros, and most other authorities. The first date which is supported by documents is 1465, in which year he is mentioned as kapellmeister at Utrecht Cathedral. A notice in Glarean's Dodecachordon quotes Erasmus as saying that he was a chorister under Obrecht at Utrecht. As Erasmus was born in 1467, and is referring to 1476, when he was nine years old, there can be nothing to make this notice incredible. We know from his lament on Okeghem that Erasmus was deeply interested in music, and that he was capable of great admiration for a musician; it would reasonably have been a matter of pride with him to have had this happy experience with Obrecht. The Utrecht period of the composer's life lasted for eighteen years, with a break of a year in 1474–5, which year he spent as a singer at the court of Hercules d'Este at Ferrara.

From 1483 to 1485 Obrecht was director of the singing-school at Cambrai. After a very brief stay at Bruges, as kapellmeister at St. Donatus, he accepted the same position at Notre Dame in Antwerp, succeeding Barbireau, as we have noted. On December 31, 1498, Obrecht returned to Bruges, and there is a notice in the Antwerp archives concerning his ill-health. Obrecht held his position in Bruges until September, 1500, without a mention of his illness; but on that date he was suddenly attacked so gravely by his malady that he asked to be relieved of his office. The dignitaries of the Chapel sympathized with his sufferings, and showed sincere grief. Seized as they were by this emergency, with no arrangements made for Obrecht's replacement, the members asked him to keep with him the pupils of the school, who could not immediately be removed; this Obrecht consented to do.

He recovered a modicum of his health, and in response to the urgent wishes of the Chapel authorities he consented to give again his precious lessons to the choirs, and to compose motets for them. In October, 1500, Obrecht was made provost of St. Peter's, Thourout, and was given the rank of chapelain. The great musician, though ill and suffering, made two more attempts at activity. He went to Antwerp again, and, in 1504, to Ferrara, where a document records his death in 1505, presumably of the plague.

Petrucci published a book of Obrecht's Masses, and included one in a collection of Masses by various composers. Single works are in various other collections of the period. Motets and hymns are to be found in the archives of the Papal Chapel and in the Royal Library at Munich. The Society for North

DUFAY TO SWEELINCK

Netherlands Music History (Vereeniging voor Noord-Nederland's Muziekgeschiedenis) undertook in 1908 the publication of Obrecht's entire compositions, under the editorship of Joh. Wolf.

Obrecht's works were very popular in his lifetime; they were sought after with utmost eagerness. Burbure tells us that the composer sent to the singers of St. Donatus in Bruges a Mass of his composing; this was in 1491; some time later the singers, grateful for the precious gift, paid him a visit at Antwerp, a visit marked by a number of banquets; the Notre Dame authorities gracefully paid the expenses.

In the artistic history of nations certain figures stand out notably in the affections of the people; sometimes this regard lasts only during the artist's lifetime; sometimes it comes into being only after they have lost the man and begun to take pride in their heritage of his fame as an artist; in rare instances the artist is appreciated while alive and also carried in the permanent affection of the people.

DUFAY TO SWEELINCK

This last was the happy fate of Jacob Obrecht. To us in Holland today he is no dry abstraction, no mere name, but a noble countryman and dear brother in art. What more beautiful destiny for an artist?

IV

JOSQUIN DEPRÈS

Josquin was born in Hainault, probably at Condé; the date has been approximately set between 1445 and 1450. In his early youth he is supposed to have been a chorister at St. Quentin. It is known that he studied with Okeghem; his Lament on the death of his master is given in full in the chapter on Okeghem. We have no details for the years immediately following Josquin's time as a student.

He appears to have been in Florence, in association with Lorenzo the Magnificent and his brilliant circle, as we learn from Aron. Josquin was already famous and "could mingle freely and pleasantly in the world of Lorenzo; he stood second to none in gifts," as Ambros writes.

Josquin went to Rome at the invitation of Pope Sixtus IV, and was for some years a member of the forces of the Papal Chapel. Authorities are in disagreement concerning the dates of the periods spent in Rome and Florence; some do not mention Florence. It is believed that Josquin went to Ferrara; at any rate, Duke Ercole commissioned him to write a composition; the work is the wonderful five-voice Miserere, a composition which ranks with Josquin's best.

Probably Josquin left Italy about 1490; we next meet him, according to many authorities, in the chapel of Louis XII of France. This monarch reigned from 1498 to 1515, but we have no means of knowing what part of that time Josquin spent at his court. Our meagre information about the period is given by Glarean. From him we learn of two small incidents.

DUFAY TO SWEELINCK

The King had promised a prebendary to the composer; Josquin, after waiting what seemed to him an undue time, reminded his royal patron of the promise; he did this by means of a passage in the 118th Psalm set to music in an interesting manner. The passage was as follows: "Memor esto verbi tui servo tuo." The other incident emphasizes the fact that Josquin enjoyed a friendly, half-confidential relation with the King. On one occasion the musician permitted himself to be ironical about the monarch's taste. The latter was very fond of a somewhat common song, humming it to himself the whole day. Josquin made a parody of the matter in a composition. This was a canon upon the song; a part, he said, was for the King, who was greatly pleased. But upon examination the royal would-be performer found that his part consisted of one unending rest! At royal birthday and nameday celebrations, however, Josquin appeared with genuine tributes in the form of compositions, "his manner of saying 'Vive le Roi!'"

Josquin returned to his homeland late in life. The date of this return we do not know, nor is it certain to which city he went. But as there has been found his deed of purchase of a house in Condé, it seems reasonable to suppose that this was his place of residence. Once established in the Netherlands, Josquin pursued with ardor his important work of teaching. Many of the gifted young composers of nearby France came to him for instruction, as well as the finest talents among his young countrymen. One could assume that such would be the case with a world-famous master like Josquin, but we have the direct testimony of Adrian Petit-Coclius.

Concerning the great number of French pupils, followers, and imitators of Josquin in the years subsequent to his eminent career, there is a witty French saying quoted by Ambros: "The gold-piece is changed into many small coins." However, Ambros speaks with fairness of the French followers of Josquin, praising their skill and elegance, though deploring the frivolity, and worse, of the texts to which they lent their talents. We shall consider the eminent Netherlands pupils of Josquin in the following chapter.

The date of Josquin's death was August 27, 1521. In his epitaph he is called Jossé Deprès. This is one of the many forms in which his name appears; others are Desprès, Deprez, Depret, Latinized as a Prato, Pratensis, in Italian as Del Prato; and Jossekin, Josquinis, Jodocus, etc.

By his contemporaries Josquin was considered the greatest master of his age; this was the opinion also of the artists of the brilliant Venetian School, voiced by Zarlino; and the musicians and writers of all the centuries since have expressed the same conviction.

Petrucci published Masses of Josquin in two editions: 1503 and 1514. Other Masses are in manuscript in the archives of the Papal Chapel, and in the libraries of Munich and Cambrai; a few are included, entire or in part, in numerous collections. Some of Josquin's most famous Masses are the *Hercules, Dux Ferrarae, L'omme armé, Fortunata desperata, Malheur me bat, De beata Virgine;* the Masses *Gaudeamus* and *Dung altre amor* are considered examples of Netherlands art at its best.

Motets were early published by Petrucci, Peutinger, and others; songs to French texts were issued by Susato of Antwerp, Attaignant in Paris, and later reprints. Many compositions have been published in modern notation in the collections of Commer, Rochlitz, etc.

Ambros, the profound musical scholar, author of the ablest history of music which we possess, made a long study of many works of Josquin; this study resulted in an admiration to which he gave enthusiastic expression.

"Not without emotion can I recollect the moment when there came into my hands the Masses of Josquin in the two editions of Petrucci. Through all the restraint of Church ritual and the art methods of that early time, there speaks in the music of Josquin a warm sensitiveness, a capacity for urgent emotion, a mystic awe of worship. His Masses are noble with the nobility of the heart's depth.

"In his other works, the abstract, elevated style of earlier composers is broken up as the undivided sunbeam is broken up by the prism into a glowing play of many colors. Here is sadness, pain, and bitter revolt; and here is intimate love, tender sympathy, and playful jest. It is an unprecedented stride forward which occurs with Josquin; in him there is 'lived through' an art development such as is found in no artist previously and in very few since."

THE AGE OF JOSQUIN

PIERRE DE LA RUE

Next in importance to Josquin during this period was Pierre de la Rue. Many of his works have survived; and although we have no records of the date and place of his birth, we possess authentic documents sufficiently consecutive to enable us to outline his career. It is known with certainty that he was a pupil of Okeghem, together with Josquin.

Eitner states that he began his long service in the Burgundian court in the year 1492, with Mary of Burgundy, and that he was a singer in the chapel; also, he adds, la Rue began his service with Philippe the Fair in 1499.

The records of Courtrai prove that he received an appointment as prebendary there in 1501.

The later researches of Van der Straeten revealed that La Rue went twice to Spain in the service of Philippe the Fair; he is found in the Chapel lists of Madrid in 1502 and 1506. A document of 1510 contains his resignation as Prebendary of St. Albans at Namur. Following this he was at the court of Margaret of Austria, Regent of the Netherlands for Maximilian.

The distinguished composer was treated by Margaret with every honor; she caused his Masses to be written in the rich codices which are now divided between the Royal Library at Brussels and the Ambraser Collection which came to Vienna among the effects of the Archduke Ferdinand.

"Margaret played the lute, and, from all evidences, the spinet. Her love for art was sincere, and her elegant residence at Mechelen was the habitual gathering-place of virtuosi. One may still see the pavilion of her princely mansion, where she listened to all kinds of performances, and the spacious hall where she entertained the most gifted musicians of her time," says Van der Straeten in "Charles Quint, musicien." "Margaret even made attempts at composition, aided by several masters in the adaptation of themes to her verses." It was under the care of Margaret that Charles V began that lifelong study and love of music which made him a figure unique among monarchs.

Pierre de la Rue died at Courtrai on November 20, 1518. He was one of the great masters of the contrapuntal style; besides his technical skill, he had qualities of noble musicianship. His work has been praised for its "strong, rejoicing spirit."

Petrucci published a volume of Masses in 1503; others are in the libraries of Brussels, Vienna, Mechelen, and Berlin, and in the Papal archives. A Mass is included in the Expert "Maîtres musiciens" of 1890. Motets and madrigals were printed in various collections, where there are also songs to French, Flemish, and Italian texts.

The composer's name appears as Pierchon, Pierson, Pierazon, and, Latinized, as Petrus Platensis.

LOUIS COMPÈRE (Loyset)

ANOTHER FELLOW-PUPIL of Okeghem with Josquin was Louis Compère, usually called Loyset. But little of his work is extant, and few details of his life are known; but the estimation of contemporaries places him among the great of his time.

Although we know with certainty that he was a pupil of Okeghem, no records exist concerning his place and date of birth. It is known that it took place in Flanders, about 1460. Scanty but authentic documents show him to have been a chorister of the Cathedral of St. Quentin; he became canon there later, and records show that he was Chancellor of the Cathedral at the time of his death. His epitaph places the date of his death on August

16, 1518, a few months previous to the death of Pierre de la Rue.

Petrucci published motets of Compère at Venice in his collections of 1501 and 1503; other motets are in his collections of 1519, published at Fossombrone, and in Petreius. Manuscript Masses are in the archives of the Papal Chapel. There are also several songs to French texts, some published, some in manuscript.

Compère has been called "the romantic composer of his time, an original character." Ambros says that his work shows deep feeling, and that his technique is rich and fine. "Eccentricity and artificiality are entirely absent."

The composer's name is Latinized as Ludovicus Compater. He is mentioned in the Lament of Josquin on Okeghem.

ANTOINE BRUMEL

BRUMEL is the remaining pupil of Okeghem mentioned by Josquin. Except for the fact of his training we know little of the life of this composer. His name in its Flemish form is Broemel; he is referred to in early writings sometimes simply as A. B.

The researches of Van der Straeten have made evident that he was in the service of the Duke of Sora at Lyons, and in Ferrara at the ducal court of Alfonso I, brother-in-law of his first patron. Brumel began his appointment with Alfonso on July 28, 1505. There are no other documents available concerning Brumel's career. The period of his life has been tentatively set between 1480 and 1520.

There are extant many Masses of Brumel: these are in collections of the time, in the Maldeghem "Trésor," the Expert "Maîtres musiciens," and in manuscript in the libraries of Rome, Vienna, and Munich. The compositions reveal sincere musical feeling as well as clarity and skill in the handling of voices.

ALEXANDER AGRICOLA

THE REAL NAME of Agricola was Ackermann, and his birth is assigned by all authorities to about 1446, in Holland. Kiesewetter and Fétis call him a pupil of Okeghem; Eitner, Ambros, and Van der Straeten do not corroborate this, but neither do they contradict it; it may be considered as probable.

Agricola was a chorister in the ducal chapel of the Sforzas at Milan; his resignation from this position is recorded in a document of June 10, 1474. He was in the service of Philippe the Fair of Burgundy about 1500, and foilowed his patron to Spain five years later. It would appear that he retained his post in the Spanish Chapel, although Philippe died within a few months of the appointment, for we find Agricola in Madrid at the court of Charles V, in 1516. It is supposed that he died between 1520 and 1530, near Valladolid, although Eitner and several other authorities do not mention these dates.

Agricola was greatly favored by Petrucci, who published a volume of songs and motets, and a book of five Masses. His work is considered by some writers to be a little heavy and at times eccentric; but all critics agree that in some of the Masses he shows great technical skill and deep feeling.

GASPAR (*Caspar van Weerbeke*)

IT IS TO VAN DER STRAETEN's discovery of several interesting documents that we owe our knowledge of the fact that this composer's name in full is Caspar van Weerbeke, and that he was born in Audenaarde. The name appears simply as Gaspar or Caspar.

He was a singer in the court chapel of Duke Galeas Sforza in Milan; the document recording this appointment in 1472 calls him "of Tournai," but it is not certain whether this means that he was born there or merely had come from there to Milan. We know that he was sent by the Duke in 1474 to Flanders to recruit for the chapel a number of the excellent Netherlands singers. This mission presumes special musical judgment, and Eitner considers that Gaspar was director of the chapel. A document of 1475 mentions, on

April 22, that the musician received a "velvet costume."

Eitner states that Gaspar was a singer in the Papal Chapel in Rome from 1481 to 1489, returning to Milan in that year. In 1490, we know from documents that he returned again to Flanders, and was greeted by his Auden-aarde admirers with many demonstrations of honor. On this occasion he was called in the records by the title of Sanghmeester (maître de chant). He made a festal entry into his native city.

It is stated by Eitner that Gaspar returned to the Papal Chapel in 1499, and that salary lists mention him until 1509; after that date there is a period in which the lists are missing. Our last documentary record of Gaspar is dated March 12, 1536; on that date he conducted a performance of twenty-two singers in honor of Pietro Aron, who entered a monastery at Bergamo on that day.

A volume of Gaspar's Masses was published by Petrucci in 1506; the same publisher issued motets, Lamentations, and a few secular songs. Manuscript Masses are in the archives of the Papal Chapel. Gafor mentions Gaspar among the most skilful composers of his time. Ambros considers his work beautiful, original, and spiritually strong.

JEAN MOUTON

JEAN MOUTON was a pupil of Josquin and the teacher of Adrian Willaert. It is believed that he was born at Holling, near Metz, because his name appeared as "Jean van Holling"; the date of his birth is not known. He was singer, or, some authorities say, maître de chapelle at the court of Louis XII and Francis I of France. Mouton became Canon of Thérouanne; on October 30, 1522, he died at St. Quentin.

It was during Mouton's Paris career that the young Willaert made his acquaintance and became his devoted pupil, abandoning the study of law. A year before his death Mouton visited Paris again; the learned and famous Glarean was there, having come from his home in Basel. A conversation between these two great men is recorded by Glarean; he states that Mouton, to accommodate himself to Glarean's convenience, spoke Latin instead of French; this impressed Glarean favorably, and he writes with enthusiasm of the culture of Mouton.

The musical eminence of Mouton is evident from his work; it reflects the finished technique and sound musical learning of the Josquin school. But Mouton was no mere follower; he was a powerful, original talent; and though the general characteristics resemble those of his teacher, his individual gifts are stamped upon every page.

"His compositions are never pedantic, but move with freedom and life," says Ambros. "Yet in the technical matter of voice-leading Mouton is in advance of every predecessor, even his master Josquin."

We possess Masses of Mouton, published by Petrucci in 1515, and in manuscript at Vienna, Cambrai, and in the Papal Archives. Songs were published by Scotto, and are in manuscript in the Imperial Library at Vienna.

ANTOINE FEVIN

THIS COMPOSER, who has been called the "shining, lovable Fevin," was a contemporary of Josquin concerning whose life we have no details whatever, but of whose work a rich heritage has come down to us. From dates and names on the title-pages of Fevin's published works it is learned that he died between the dates of February 24, 1514 and January 23, 1516. The writings of Glarean speak of his death at an early age, probably at twenty-four or -five. It is believed that Josquin was his teacher, but this is not based upon documentary facts.

"In any case it is certain that Josquin was his example, whom he emulated, not in a poor imitation, or in borrowing another's leavings, but as one noble spirit pays homage to another noble one. Fevin was a richly gifted artist; his works are full of the fire of genius, and are of a

ripe mastery although he died so young."
Thus writes Ambros; and Glarean says that
he "knows hardly anything more charming
in sound than the Mass, 'Ave Maria.'"

Masses by Fevin were published by Petrucci
in 1515, by Antiquiis in 1516, and are in manuscript in the Imperial Library at Vienna.
Motets are in the Petrucci "Motetti della
corona" of 1514, and in other collections.
French chansons are in collections dated 1540
and 1545.

NOËL BAULDEWIJN

THIS COMPOSER was a Netherlander of the 15th
century; a few dates tell us something of his
career, and we possess some of his work. He
was first a singer at Notre Dame, Antwerp;
then, from 1513 to 1518, maître de chapelle at
the Ste. Vierge; he died about 1530. The name
appears under the forms Baulduin, Baudoin,
Baldewin, Valduin, and is Latinized as Natalis
Balduinis.

Two of his motets are in Petrucci's "Motetti della corona," 1519, and others are in different collections. Manuscript Masses are in Rome and Munich. Eitner states that this composer must not be confused with Jehan Baudewyn, who lived at the same time; the latter was a singer in the Spanish Chapel of Charles V.

JACOTIN

BURBURE, quoted by Eitner, states that Jacotin was a name used by Jacob Godebrie, or Jacques Godebrye, Latinized in documents as Jacobus Godefridus. On July 9, 1479, he received a benefice at Notre Dame, Antwerp, where he was engaged as singer. He kept this connection until his death, the approximate date of which is probably indicated by the appointment of his successor on March 24, 1528. Another Jacotino, born in Picardy, is mentioned in a Document of 1474 as singer at the ducal chapel in Milan.

Eitner raises the question, which cannot be answered at present: which of these is the composer of the works bearing the name Jacotin? These are in sixteenth century collections and in manuscript at Leyden; they consist of songs and madrigals.

JOHANNES TINCTORIS

A MUSICIAN OF IMPORTANCE in this period is Tinctoris. As a composer he has left work which would merit remembrance; but his fame rests upon his achievements as a theorist and writer. He was born in 1446, probably at Poperinghe.

Of his career we know but little. He was chapelain and singer at the court of Ferdinand of Aragon at Naples in 1476, and founded in that city one of the earliest conservatories of music. A list dated October 10, 1480, mentions him still as singer in the chapel. A document of October 15, 1487, gives us the information that Tinctoris was sent by the King to engage singers for the chapel. He went north for the purpose, but did not return to Naples.

It is believed by some authorities, including

Haberl, that Tinctoris spent some time as a member of the Papal Chapel in the time of Pope Alexander VI; there is, however, nothing to prove this.

Tinctoris returned to the Netherlands, and died at Nivelles; he was canon there at the time. The document which mentions the appointment of his successor is dated October 12, 1511, and this is taken as the approximate date of his death. Eitner states that Tinctoris was at one time canon at Évreux.

A famous work of Tinctoris is the "Terminorum musicae diffinitorium," published at Naples in 1475, and reprinted by Coussemaker in his "Scriptores." Tinctoris was the author also of "Liber de natura et proprietate tonorum," dedicated to Okeghem and Busnois jointly, and of the much-quoted "Ars contrapuncti," which was written, according to Van der Straeten, in 1476, or, in the opinion of Brenet, in 1477. A number of other treatises were written later, and have been edited by Coussemaker.

DUFAY TO SWEELINCK

Songs by Tinctoris are in the Petrucci collections, and there are manuscripts in the libraries of Milan, Verona, and St. Gall.

VI

THE VENETIAN SCHOOL

ADRIAN WILLAERT is
one of the glories of Netherlands art. He had
great natural gifts, which he used with
judgment and diligence for the noblest pur-
poses. His own career was so brilliant and his
compositions so great that it would seem that
nothing could add a further distinction to his
name. But Willaert has a share in yet another
honor; he is one of that sequence of geniuses
which links modern musical history firmly
to the Netherlands masters. He was the
faithful pupil of Mouton, as Mouton was of
Josquin, Josquin of Okeghem and Okeghem of
Dufay; and he was the painstaking teacher of

Zarlino and Gabrieli, as they were the teach-
ers of Sweelinck, and Sweelinck of the magnificent group of North German musicians to
whose principles and traditions we owe Johann
Sebastian Bach. The line is straight and plain
and strong, and it begins with two hundred
years of Netherlands' supremacy.

Willaert was born in Rousselaere (Roulers),
West Flanders, between 1488 and 1490; this is
considered definite by both Grégoir and Van
der Straeten, the two authorities who have
devoted special research to the life of Willaert.
The composer was intended by his parents for
the law; as there were no law-schools nearby,
Adrian was sent by his family to Paris, like
many other Flemish youths destined for legal
or scientific careers. This was about 1514.

At that time there lived in Paris a gifted
Netherlands artist, Jean Mouton, maître de
chapelle of Louis XII, and pupil of the great
Josquin. Willaert made his acquaintance; it is
easy to imagine the two talented countrymen
together, and the influence of the fine, sincere

man upon the enthusiastic youth. Mouton began to teach Willaert, and from that time forward we hear no more of legal study. Willaert spent some years in Paris.

From Paris he went to Rome. While there he heard, in August, 1518, a performance in one of the churches of the hymn, "Verbum bonum et suave," which he himself had composed in Paris; it was being sung under the name of Josquin. Upon his making known to the singers the identity of the composer, they refused to sing the work again. This anecdote is given by Grégoir; and Van der Straeten, in volume six of the "Musique aux Pays-Bas," quotes Zarlino, who heard it, "maintes fois," from Willaert himself. This composition was later published by Petrucci in the "Motetti della corona."

It appears that Willaert remained but a short time in Rome, and that he made at this time a brief visit to Venice; we soon find him at the court of Ludwig, King of Bohemia and Hungary. Ludwig was killed in the battle of

Mohacs in 1526, and thus the composer's position at his court was ended. But Willaert's compositions were beginning to be known and his name to be honored to such an extent that he was appointed late in 1527 to the position of maestro di capella at San Marco in Venice. This was at that time a very important musical post.

Willaert brought to his new duties an untiring zeal; he composed a great deal, and achieved so eminent and widespread a reputation that the finest talents came to him for instruction. Among the pupils of Willaert in Venice were Cyprien de Rore, famous composer and the immediate successor of Willaert at San Marco; Gioseffo Zarlino, the distinguished theorist; Constanzo Porta of Cremona, a musician of wide influence in Italy; Andrea Gabrieli and his nephew Giovanni, who were among the foremost musicians of the time both as organists and composers; Girolamo Parabosco, a great organist of Parma; and Léonard Barré of Limoges, composer and singer in the Papal Chapel in 1555. The renowned Venetian School grew up around the personal teaching of Willaert. Of Zarlino we read in Ambros that "his works are famous from his day to our own, works as full of understanding, as profound, as they are elegant and ably written." The Gabrielis had to thank Willaert for their entire training. Sweelinck, as was mentioned, was a pupil in organ-playing of Andrea Gabrieli and in composition of Zarlino.

Willaert created the style of composition which made use of two or more choirs; it is probable that the placement of the two organs at San Marco suggested this. The beauty of Willaert's own compositions for divided and answering choirs, organs, and other instruments, and the wonderful effects produced by the works of his famous associates inspired the Roman School of composers to adopt this style.

"As the Venetian painters suffused their work with a transfiguring light, so the Vene-

tian composers achieved marvels of lovely
sound with the colorful interplay of anti-
phonal choirs, and later with the mingling of
glowing instrumental tones. The church music
of Gabrieli, with its answering choirs and
its accompanying strings and trombones, is to
music what an Assumption of Titian is to
painting," writes Ambros, who rejoices to
find such analogies. We shall recall this also
in his mention of Breughel and Callot in connection with other composers.

Besides his important and far-reaching in-
novations in the composition of church-
music, Willaert has the distinction of being
the first of the great madrigalists. "The
madrigal, as we know, appears with Francesco Landino in the fourteenth century;
but it emerges for the first time as a beloved
and widespread music-form under Willaert,
to whom it is not without justice assigned
as his own creation," we learn from Ambros.
A madrigal meant originally a shepherd's
song, from mandriale, whose root is man-

dra (a flock). The madrigal availed itself
of contrapuntal treatment suggested by the
motet, and became a beautiful art-form. M.
Suremonet tell us that Fétis produced at Brussels in 1846 a six-voiced madrigal of Willaert;
"despite the hundreds of years since its composition, it was impressive and beautiful to
us."

Grégoir, in his Dutch monograph on Willaert, mentions a painting by Hamman; this
represents Willaert conducting a performance
in the palace of the Doge. "Willaert is seated
at a small organ, surrounded by singing
monks; an audience of nobles and ladies is
seen. It is a lively and interesting picture."

The love and reverence of the Venetians for
Willaert knew no bounds. The writings of his
contemporaries are aflame with true enthusiasm; he was called the prince of music, the
pride of Venice, the phoenix; his compositions and their performance at San Marco
were called "drinkable gold" (oro potabile).
Poems were written in his honor; his manu-

scripts were treasured in the archives as if, as was indeed true, they were more precious than jewels. He was called "Maestro Adriano," or, with deep popular affection, merely "Adriano."

This homage was the more amazing in that "the ground-tone of Venetian feeling was a proud, yes, a contemptuous isolation, with a resultant inner solidarity," writes Jacob Burckhardt. Ambros says: "The official musical positions, such as organist and maestro di capella at San Marco, had until then been filled by Venetians. Only an authoritative personal dictum by the artistically enlightened Doge Andrea Gritti made possible the appointment of a Netherlander. The northern master retrieved with amazing quickness the previous delinquencies of musical Venice, and placed her far beyond her rivals, Rome and Florence. Venice's music rose unexpectedly in magnificence and beauty from the sea. It needed a Palestrina and his colleagues to wrest ascendancy from her and place it in Rome."

DUFAY TO SWEELINCK

The great musician, thus adored and honored in his adopted home, preserved during his whole life a deep love for his native land. Twice he made the long and fatiguing journey there from Venice; we see in the records of San Marco his leaves of absence, dated March 31, 1542, and May 8, 1556. In Willaert's later years he cherished a plan for returning to the Netherlands to live in quiet retirement, but he was persuaded by his friends and by his own reason to remain to the end in Venice, the theatre of his glorious career. He died there December 7, 1562.

We possess numerous madrigals, motets, and songs of Willaert, and a few Masses. These were published by Phalèse, Susato, LeRoy and Ballard, Gardano and Scotto, and in various collections and reprints. Manuscripts are in the libraries of Brussels, Vienna, Cambrai, and in the Papal archives.

VII

NETHERLANDS MASTERS THROUGHOUT EUROPE IN THE SIXTEENTH CENTURY

T**HE EARLY NETHER-LANDS MASTERS** and those of the time of Josquin were appreciated throughout their own land, and were welcomed and honored in the highest offices of great cathedrals and princely courts in other countries as well. In the sixteenth century we have seen the splendor of Netherlands musical art as fostered by the wealthy and cultured Venetians, and we shall consider in a later chapter the powerful influence of Orlande de Lassus in Munich; here it is our plan to follow the other Netherlands artists who, with Lassus and the Venetian School, were the glory of all Europe during that period.

PHILIPPE DE MONTE

ONE OF THE MOST INTERESTING of these is Philippe de Monte. His extant works are numerous, and details regarding his career have come down to us with exceptional completeness. The principal sources of the biographical data are: the unusually full and explicit records of the Imperial Chapel at Vienna; the "Dictionnaire des artistes de la Bohème" by Dlabacz, librarian in a monastery at Prague; the inscriptions on a portrait by the artist Sadeler at Prague in 1594; and a long Latin poem in honor of de Monte.

The date of his birth is given by Dlabacz as 1521; the date as indicated on the portrait is 1517. His birthplace was Mechelen. This is made conclusive by the list of the personnel of the Imperial Chapel for 1582, which calls him "Philippe de Monte of Malines." Also we have the statement of Dlabacz that he was born at Mechelen. A few writers have tried to find in his name some indication that he was born at Mons but this is referred to by Van der Straeten as follows: "In the sixteenth century the names of places had already long been used as surnames, and the bearers had dispersed so widely that it is not reasonable to base any assumptions, otherwise unfounded, on his name alone." Doorslaer, a serious student of de Monte, and himself a Malinois, considers the matter beyond dispute.

Philippe de Monte was in early life maître de chapelle at Cambrai; later he enjoyed a non-resident canonicat there. He was appointed kapellmeister of the Imperial Chapel at Vienna under Maximilian II in 1568, receiving a salary of thirty florins a month; this seems to have been the usual amount given to eminent musicians there, for we read that Jacques de Buus received a like sum. In the beginning of his incumbency de Monte shared this position with Jacques Vaet; his exclusive functioning dates from 1577.

The Imperial Chapel had at this period eighty-three members, maîtres, vice-maîtres, singers, and players of various instruments forming a list of high merit. Documents relative to the arrangements made for these musicians show that the influence of the Netherlanders was supreme, an influence at once artistic, administrative, and practical.

This brilliant period of de Monte's life was succeeded by his remarkable career at Prague. The first documentary date concerning this is of 1593, but it is clearly evident that he went to Prague several years before that date. The document in question mentions the composition by de Monte of a work in honor of the inauguration of an archbishop at Prague. The portrait by Sadeler, dated 1594, shows us the musician at seventy-two years of age, "revealing a short, good-natured face, surmounted by a tall, extremely ugly cap," says Ambros. This cap, Van der Straeten tells us, was that of the Imperial Court of Rudolph at Prague.

At this time there lived in Prague a remarkable woman, Elizabeth Weston. She had been born in England, but had removed to Prague in early life, secured an education in the classics which enabled her to write excellent Latin poetry, and won by her intelligence and loyalty many friends among the artistic circles of Rudolph's court. She took lessons of de Monte, became his friend, and admired him with an understanding enthusiasm. She wrote a long Latin poem as a tribute to de Monte; it begins as follows:

> Amphion tu mollis, tu cantu numinis iram,
> Orpheus tu lapides, imo Acheronta moves,
> Caesaris hoc mecum Rudolphi tota fatetur
> Aula, nec hoc ipsum splendida Roma negat,
> Gallia te celebrat, te tellus Italia laudat,
> Ingeniique tui cantat Iberus opes.

Elizabeth Weston mentions in this poem her study with de Monte. She treats at length and with fervor of the honor in which he was held by the court of Rudolph; of the admiration of Rome for de Monte's work; of the praises of all Italy for the "Belgian Orpheus"; of his fame in France and in Spain. She finishes with the hope that the whole world will continue to pay him the homage which he deserves.

The poem is based upon fact, both as regards de Monte's widespread fame and his artistic merit. Human nature being what it is, we may suppose that there were those among the contemporary readers of Elizabeth's poem who considered it a grave error for her to record so many merits, but the scholars of succeeding centuries have taken this tribute very seriously indeed.

The published works of de Monte are everywhere numerous. Ambros gives a list which includes nineteen books of madrigals, French songs, settings of Ronsard's Sonnets, five books of motets for five voices, motets for six and for twelve voices, and two books of Masses. The Hawkins history and the collections of Dehn and Commer contain each a work. Ambros considers de Monte's compositions "Beautifully written, with great skill and originality, though the latter results from no straining after something new merely for the sake of novelty. He is one of the musicians who throw a glowing light on Netherlands art."

From the "Kaiserliche Hof-Musikkapell in Wien" by van Köchel we learn the date of de Monte's death as given by the Imperial records; this date was July 4, 1603. A long, brilliant, and fruitful career was his.

JACOB CLEMENS

THIS GREAT MUSICIAN, often called Clemens non Papa to distinguish him from Pope Clement VII, has left us a wealth of compositions. But almost no details of his life have been found, in spite of extensive and painstaking research. We are able to assign the period of his career, because an elegy on his death, by Jacques Vaet, is dated 1558, and Hermann Finck speaks of him as still living in 1556. With these exceptions we have no dates.

Fétis and others believe, on account of the

Vaet elegy (Vaet having lived in Vienna),
that Clemens was in Imperial service under
Charles V. There is no documentary basis for
this, and Eitner remarks cautiously that "it
seems he was in Imperial service." Walther's
Lexicon calls him "a Netherlander and the
most highly considered composer of Charles
V." On the contrary, Ambros, so thoroughly
informed on all matters relating to Vienna, is
convinced that Clemens never went there; he
believes that he remained in the Netherlands.

Clemens' works were published at about
the date of his death by two of the most important Netherlands music publishers, Phalèse
and Tilman (Tielman) Susato. The former issued many Masses, a large number of motets,
volumes of secular songs, etc.; Susato published the remarkable "Soeter liedekins," arrangements of the Psalms which were very
popular. In the Commer collection Clemens
is represented by several motets.

Ambros considers the songs of Clemens "the
fairest blossoms which the Netherlands' art

has produced in this field. And looking over
its extent, from Dufay's 'Ce moys de May,'
from the songs of Okeghem and Binchois,
through Josquin and Compère to Clemens, one
wins a view of genial development which it is
impossible to see without interest, sympathy,
and admiration." Concerning the motets he
writes: "They may serve as examples of the
purest motet style; they have a noble beauty
of motive, a glowing richness of harmony, and
a tonal structure as skilful as it is artistic.

"In the six-part 'Santa Barbara' motet and
in one for seven voices, Clemens employs a
grouping of high and low voices in a dia-
logue form so entirely in the manner and style
of Palestrina that one has to be reminded that
it is not Palestrina indeed, but a composer
from before his time. Palestrina is entirely
foreshadowed. We must cease bringing up on
the carpet the old errors and fables concerning
'degenerate music'; we must learn what manner of man this was, what manner of men and
artists were his glorious countrymen; we must

rejoice with our whole souls in the continuous development of a pure, beautiful art of music."

This brings us to a matter which cannot be avoided in a study of Netherlands musicians of the sixteenth century. This period found all Europe, for the first time, taking a deep and active interest in music *as an art*. Not as folk-song, not as folk dance-tune, not as subservient improvisation to accompany the tale of minstrel or troubadour, not even any longer solely as handmaid to religious service, but as the highest and most noble of the arts did music take its place throughout Europe during the culminating years of the Renaissance.

Admittedly it was, however, dependent to a great extent upon the Church for countenance and support, and upon her ritual for inspiration and text. And the Church felt this to be a grave responsibility, especially where it touched her actual devotions.

In the same way that the B minor Mass of Bach is too highly wrought, too absorbing

in its artistry to be suited to use in actual
church service, while it is, nevertheless, a
towering work of art as eminently conducive
to noble and elevated thought as it is plainly
the product of such thought, in the same way,
let us repeat, the work of the Netherlands
masters grew, by reason of its intricate beauty,
its too absorbing artistic interest, to be un-
suited to the devotional exercise of the
Church's ritual. The Church of Rome has
never "condemned" the B minor Mass of
Bach; the idea is preposterous; in earlier
times, in the same way, she likewise never
"condemned" the Masses of Obrecht and Josquin, of Clemens, Arcadelt, and Lassus.

Quite wisely the Church decided that a
simpler music should be used at the celebration of Mass; quite sincerely she strove to find
the type of music best fitted to direct the attention of the worshipper to the meaning and
spirit of the Mass rather than to its artistic
setting. This was the whole matter at issue in
the so-called "reform" of church music.

That fact must be clearly borne in mind. Almost wholly unfounded are the oft-quoted calumnies regarding songs used as Mass-themes by pre-Palestrina composers; for instance, the ignorant statements of Berlioz are mere parrot-like repetitions of these calumnies, without support of a single specific example or quotation, for the excellent reason that he had made no study of the subject upon which he presumed to hold forth. There are other instances of an ignorance as profound and audacious. Few indeed are the examples in which songs composed originally to unseemly texts were used as themes for Masses; and these examples, without exception, concern minor composers, mediocrities, who in the middle ages contrived, as such still contrive, to creep into places where they bring discredit upon their betters. Not indecency, not "degeneracy," but a too-absorbing artistic interest was the cause of the change in Church ritual music.

But this change during the late sixteenth

century was seized upon by misguided or interested elements within the Church, and later by ignorant or unscrupulous elements among her enemies, and was made a pretext for the belittling and smirching of some of the most glorious works of art ever produced by man.

Valiantly, and valiantly sponsored and financed by the "Society of Friends of Music" of Catholic Vienna, the eminent Ambros labored in the just cause of refuting such error, supporting his testimony with exhaustive and authentic quotations from the works themselves and from Church documents of the most impressive fullness and clarity; and valiantly have other learned musicians and sound churchmen toiled and quoted and demonstrated in the cause of silencing these fantastic legends. All this effort has been rewarded; today it requires an exceptionally benighted or bigoted writer, aided by a publisher of the same status, to bring forward "the old errors" in fresh effrontery. It does happen occasionally, however; we must therefore continue each to add a word on the side of artistic truth and justice.

JACOB ARCADELT

ONE OF THE NETHERLANDS MUSICIANS who had great influence in Italy was Arcadelt. We know from the records of the Julian Chapel that he was choirmaster there in 1539. In December, 1540, he is recorded as singer there; in 1544 he received the office of Abbas or Camerlingo. Arcadelt is cited in the daily records of the Chapel until 1549. He was frequently ill, and the records note many absences.

From the title-pages of his printed Masses we learn that Arcadelt was, in 1557, in the service of Cardinal Charles of Lorraine, who resided in Paris until 1560. According to the known dates, it seems that Arcadelt had an active career of about thirty-six years; that he was born around 1514 in Flanders, and died some time after 1557 in Paris.

[95]

Arcadelt wrote a large number of compositions, some of them of such quality that they give him a high place among the musicians of that age. With Willaert he was one of the founders of the madrigal genre. Among his published works are six books of these, and they are considered his finest compositions. They were published in Venice between 1538 and 1556. The first book of Arcadelt's madrigals, issued in 1538, had such a success that it had to be reprinted in no less than sixteen closely following editions! An almost unexampled success. The five other books followed, as noted, within a few years.

Three books of Masses were published by LeRoy and Ballard in Paris in 1557. Ambros considers that they have "vitality, noble sentiment, and manliness, and are masterworks of composition." Modern collections by Riemann, Maldeghem, and others contain single works. Many motets in manuscript are in various libraries. The very famous "Ave Maria" usually attributed to Arcadelt may be his work, but Eitner and Van der Straeten doubt that it is so.

CYPRIEN DE RORE

"DURING THE MOST FLOURISHING PERIOD of Mechelen, under the magnificent Margaret of Austria, Regent of the Netherlands, who held her brilliant court in that city, it was the birthplace of Cyprien de Rore, one of the celebrated contrapuntists." Thus writes Raymond van Aerde, fellow-townsman of de Rore. We possess many works of de Rore and considerable authentic material about his career.

His name may have been an Italianized form of Van den Dauw. Rabelais, in his Pantagruel, calls him Rouzée, the archaic form of rosée (dew). His birth is placed by all authorities in 1516. Mechelen, the court city at that time, was a center of artistic and intellectual activity, and educational standards were naturally high. It is supposed that de Rore was a pupil at St. Rombaut's maîtrise.

It is known that musical education in any of the good maîtrises (Church establishments) during the sixteenth century in the Netherlands was no sinecure. Van Aerde says: "It comprised two periods; the first commenced at eight or nine years of age, when the student began as choir-boy; he learned solmisation, the aridities of proportional notation, the difficulties of white notation; he received instruction in the first principles of singing, for his voice must mix with those of the other singers in the solemn ceremonies. Arrived at the age of change of voice, our future musician entered the second stage of study; in this he learned harmony, counterpoint, canon, and composition. De Rore must have been a diligent student. We know that he began very early to keep a note-book in which he set down his ideas; this habit became a fixed one, and the little book his familiar friend."

We do not know the date of de Rore's departure for Italy, but it must have been previous to 1542, because the printing of some of his work at Venice is dated then. He was a pupil of Adrian Willaert, and he carried to this great opportunity the industrious habits of his boyhood. He began to compose when very young, and received publication promptly, which must mean that he early achieved a reputation in Italy.

In 1553 de Rore was offered the position of maître de chapelle to Duke Hercules IV of Ferrara; doubtless the influence of Willaert heiped to secure this. De Rore made an excellent impression in this position, and was given a fine house and paid a generous salary. He remained five years; at the end of that time he asked for leave of absence as he wished to visit his parents in Mechelen.

The composer found his native city in revolt and his parents fled to Antwerp, where he followed them. After some months he wished to return to Ferrara, and sent a letter asking permission to resume his duties. No reply was received, and within a year Duke Hercules died. De Rore had intended to pass the rest of his life in his native land, but the condition of the country made it necessary to seek employment elsewhere. He applied to the son of Duke Hercules in another letter, but again there was no reply. Orlande de Lassus was at that time passing through the Netherlands to engage artists for Duke Albert of Bavaria, and he took de Rore with him to Munich.

It is difficult to understand why de Rore did not remain in Munich, but such is the case. He returned again to Antwerp, where he suffered poverty and discouragement which affected his spirits and his health. At last he secured the offer of a position in Parma, as choirmaster to Prince Farnese; he accepted "feverishly," Van Aerde says, and Farnese sent the money for the journey. At Parma he remained two years, and then received the greatest honor of his life, being asked to succeed Willaert at San Marco in Venice. There he received a generous salary and a residence, yet he stayed only eighteen months!

No one understands the reasons for these

extraordinary flights of de Rore from honorable and prosperous positions. The San Marco appointment was gladly taken by Zarlino, and de Rore returned to Parma, where he died in 1565. He is buried in the Cathedral there. His death was hastened by the unhappy vicissitudes of his life, by the grief which he felt for the difficulties of his parents and his country, and by an almost continual anxiety about money.

Ambros calls de Rore "the first-born of Willaert's Venetian School." It is certain that he received training of the highest excellence, and made the most of it in developing his talent. His work belongs to the best of his time.

The most famous publishers of Italy, France, and the Netherlands printed the compositions of de Rore: Gardano and Scotto of Venice published a large number of motets, madrigals, and other works; LeRoy and Ballard of Paris issued a large book of Masses in four, five, and six voices, and two Passion settings; motets and madrigals appeared in the collections of Phalèse of Louvain and Susato of Antwerp. In manuscript in the Munich Library are Masses, madrigals, and motets.

The madrigal genre suited de Rore's manner of thought and feeling; he is in fact one of the most genial and gifted of all the madrigalists. His nature was warm, earnest, and sensitive, and his music reflects these qualities.

The awakening interest in chromatics at that time caused de Rore to experiment with their use in a group of madrigals; these were published by Gardano in five books, between 1560 and 1568. De Rore and the others of his time did not have a true grasp of the problems of chromatics, and these pieces show that they are experiments, and not always happy in results. But such experiments had to be made, and it is to the composer's credit that he took the interest and made the effort which these works clearly show.

A beautiful memorial to de Rore is that of Duke Albert V of Bavaria, the famous luxe-codex in the Munich Library, containing motets, and embellished by a portrait of the musician by Johann Mielich. A statue was erected in de Rore's honor in 1863 by the city of Mechelen; it stands in the entrance of the city-hall of this his dearly loved birthplace, to revisit which he twice sacrificed security and honors.

NICOLAS GOMBERT

A NETHERLANDS MUSICIAN whom we delight to study is Gombert. Many of his works are preserved for us, and his career is known in some detail, as is also that of his imperial patron.

Gombert was born at Bruges about 1495, and was one of the most gifted pupils of Josquin. Records of 1530 show him in the service of Charles V in the Imperial Chapel at Madrid, and there he remained until his peaceful retirement to his native land, where he died some time after 1570. His retirement was made possible by the generosity of the emperor.

As the whole career of Gombert is bound up with the musical interest of Charles, we may here permit ourselves the pleasure of recalling that the monarch was for many years not only the "absolute arbiter of Europe," but also Europe's most discriminating and most lavish patron of music, and this for the reason that he was himself a musician of such gifts and training as make him unique in history.

The very first moments of Charles' life are connected with beautiful sounds; "when he was born the carillons of the populous city of Ghent were rung in celebration." In "Charles Quint, musicien," Van der Straeten writes: "His childhood at Mechelen was the most harmonious possible; in the salons of the Archduchess Margaret he made his first childish acquaintance with the spinet.

"We remember with pleasure that in those days they decorated the keyed instruments in the most charming manner, and we may be certain that the instruments destined for princely use were made as beautiful as possible;

every effort was made to surround the children of such households with light and gayety. Even their small carriages and wagons were decorated with the greatest taste."

As Charles grew older he became a docile and deeply attentive student of music, and it was apparent that he was extraordinarily gifted. He first studied with the organist Van Vijven, and then with Bredemers. "The finesse of Charles' taste, so much praised by Sandoval, was evident even through the immaturity of youth." The early interest in the spinet continued, and Charles studied the organ and musical theory. Bredemers arranged his studies with the utmost care and thoroughness, realizing that he had to do with a genuine talent.

The musical treasures accumulated by Philippe the Good were inherited by Charles, and certain books came to him as the heir of Charles of Croy; Margaret of York left him a further legacy of the kind. In the library of his aunt, Margaret of Austria, he had access to "the splendors of Flemish musical calligraphy." Later, in his own personal library, he put musical calligraphers at work, this interest being the result of the countless observations and assiduous studies which he made throughout the years when he had at his disposal so many marvels of art in ornamented notation.

Charles loved the Netherlands, and all through the glories of the imperial reign he carried the deep and abiding affection, always spending as much time there as the exigencies of his life made possible. And, as we know, he thankfully laid down his crowns at last, in order that he might remain there in peace and quietness, living only for music and the practice of devotion.

And as he loved the Netherlands, so Charles loved the music of the Netherlands, and the artists who made this music possible. From his earliest youth he was enraptured by the sound of the great works of Netherlands composers as they were given in the Cathedral at

Mechelen. And when he became emperor, with sumptuous courts in Vienna, Spain, and the Netherlands, he placed his distinguished countrymen in the highest positions in the chapels which he maintained at these courts; the compositions of these musicians and their compatriots were performed daily, and the singers and the players of the many instruments were, as far as possible, from his native land. Charles was a mighty force in the history of his time, and in the history of the music of that time.

At the head of the Madrid Chapel was Nicolas Gombert. Ambros says that "the noble Gombert clearly belongs among the great masters of music; one sees throughout his work that he is the spiritual heir of Josquin, yet gifted for the creating of new treasures. His work is original and beautiful; yet it is counterpoint, full, impressive, Netherlands counterpoint with which we have here to do. And the same artist who writes his Masses and motets in so elevated a style knows how to be simple and lovable in his songs.''

A very remarkable piece of Gombert's is the "Chant des Oiseaux," published in Susato's "Sammlung." It is done with a childlike and artless joy in all the twittering and trilling and calling. "In the heart of the Netherlanders lies a vivid interest in the form and character of animals; one thinks, for example, of the fine and loving treatment of nature in the 'Bird-Congress' of Breughel, and in many works of Rubens. What these his countrymen tried to express in color Gombert tries to express in tones. His skill and taste are shown in the fact that he uses only three voices; he does not wish to overpower and confuse the listener with an excess of twittering. The result is like a call of spring happiness." This estimate by Ambros is as beautiful in its way as the subject about which he is writing.

In the church music of Gombert we find, according to Fétis, "a forerunner of Palestrina." Hermann Finck states that he is a

composer who differs definitely and funda-
mentally from those who preceded him. Most
of his extant works are in the form of Masses,
motets, and songs, published by Susato of
Antwerp, Scotto of Venice, and others, and
in manuscript.

Gombert directed the music for the Spanish
coronation of Charles, and wrote a new composition for the occasion. This, we learn, was
very well executed by the members of the
chapel. We may imagine with what affectionate enthusiasm these Netherlanders strove to
honor their illustrious countryman and fellow-
musician.

Gombert was made Prebendary at Tournai
in 1534, according to Eitner; it was probably
in the enjoyment of a continuation or a re-
newal of this office that he passed his later
years.

HENRI BREDEMERS

A MUSICAL FIGURE of special interest to us at
this point is Henri Bredemers, whom we have

noted as the teacher of Charles V. He had been organist to Charles' father, Philippe the Fair, and was appointed teacher of Philippe's children by their guardian, Margaret of Austria.

"In the center of the charming group presented by the boy Charles and his sisters, Eleanor, Elizabeth, Marie (of Hungary), and Catherine, one sees the sympathetic and intelligent face of Master Bredemers," writes Van der Straeten. "He possessed a talent which adapted itself at need to either great or small affairs; and he gave the utmost care to the teaching of the royal children, while being one of the forces active in sending Netherlands musicians into all the countries of Europe.

"Together and separately the children were taught the different instruments, the lute, the viol, the spinet, and organ. To Charles Bredemers later taught musical theory and composition.

"Bredemers assisted at the birth of the art of playing the spinet, and was one of the earliest virtuosi of mark. He was able to impart to his distinguished pupils his own facility in using the resources of this polyphonic precursor of the piano. He had an insinuating gentleness, a sincerity and yet a persuasiveness which made his vogue immediate and lasting."

It is possible that Bredemers was born at Lierre, but more probable that it was at Antwerp, where he was organist at the Cathedral before passing into the service of Philippe the Fair. He was called Henri of Namur, from a Namur benefice given him by Charles. Eitner and Van der Straeten believe that he received his education from Barbingaut, the predecessor of Obrecht at Notre Dame, Antwerp. As a boy Bredemers was among the choristers of this church, as indicated by a list dated 1488. He was organist there for only a short time, being appointed in 1501 and passing the same year into the service of the Burgundian court.

Bredemers went to Spain, and accompanied Charles V to England in 1520; at Canterbury he gave a banquet to the chapel singers of Henry VIII. Everywhere he upheld, proud and high, the glory of Netherlands musical art.

We possess no compositions known to be his. The loss of his church music is greatly to be regretted, and also that of his pieces for various instruments. "A Flemish song, transcribed in tablature for the use of Charles or Eleanor — how interesting to find!"

MATTHEUS LE MAISTRE

SOME INTERESTING WORKS of Le Maistre are known to us, and a few facts concerning his career. It is certain that he was born in the Netherlands and educated there, but we have no information regarding his early life. His most famous composition, though not the worthiest, was the "Battaglia Taliana"; from the title-page of this we learn that he was in 1552 maestro di capella at Milan Cathedral.

In 1554 he appears in documents of the Royal Saxon State Archives at Dresden as kapellmeister to the Elector Augustus. The court chapel was called "Cantorey," and was an old, honorable institution, enjoying the care and support of art-loving patrons. Le Maistre remained more than fourteen years at this post. During his later life he was frequently ill and suffering, and repeatedly asked to be relieved of his duties. The composer was granted the desired retirement, with a pension, in 1568; he died in January, 1577.

The best compositions which Le Maistre has left are the songs. Of these, the German songs of 1577 and the intricate, many-voiced songs of 1566 are considered the finest examples of his work. Many of these were published by Montanus and Neuber of Nuremberg; motets and offices, as well as the "Battaglia," were also published. In manuscript at Munich are several songs, many offices, and three Masses.

CLÉMENT JANNEQUIN

ALTHOUGH IT IS POSSIBLE that Jannequin may have been French by birth, it is believed by

most authorities that he was born in the
Netherlands and that he was a pupil of Josquin, approximately contemporary with Gombert. With Gombert and Le Maistre, Jannequin was among the earliest of the composers
of so-called "program-music." But whereas
Gombert wrote with restraint and delicacy,
without striving for realism, Jannequin used
robust humor and a high degree of skill in
imitation. Ambros calls him "a veritable child
of the world, with a rare gift for genre-writ-
ing, a lively fancy, and originality."

"In a long môtet he depicts the street tu-
mult of old Paris; the themes are the cries of
the street vendors. In this charivari, each
strives to outshout the others; the half-sing-
ing tone, the strange rhythmic accents with
which sellers call their wares appear in the
different motives, such as that of the fried-
fish vendor, the faggot seller, the peddler of
shoes, and others. Each of these has his
particular 'cadenza,' recognizable from afar,
and all these form a rollicking comedy which

must vastly have diverted the Parisians of that day, accustomed to hearing these cries in their streets.

"As we paralleled the bird-motet of Gombert with a painting by Breughel, so we may here recall the engravings of Jacques Callot, in which the figures and incidents of a market-fair are set forth; laughable situations are depicted, such as the donkey's desiring to prance just when in dangerous proximity to the glass-maker's wares, etc. Jannequin enjoys writing some such fantasy."

The "Bataille" compositions of Jannequin were very popular and were often reprinted. The many imitative effects in these works, achieved entirely with human voices, are astoundingly skilful and realistic, and — given a good performance — they are remarkably effective. A whole generation of battle-pieces was engendered by these works; we have seen that Le Maistre succumbed to the temptation of popular success, and many other composers did the same. They usually selected for depiction some battle in which a patron had made a good figure.

The church compositions of Jannequin are, as may be imagined, of more vigor and originality than value. A setting of the Proverbs of Solomon in French rhyme, and one of several Psalms were published in 1554 and 1559 respectively. Several battle-pieces, a "Chant des Oiseaux," and many chansons are extant. Among the publishers of Jannequin's compositions were Attaignant of Paris and Gardano of Venice.

JACQUES DE BUUS

JACQUES DE BUUS, according to his gifted contemporaries, was an organ virtuoso of the first rank, and he has left us compositions which assure him a marked place among the musicians of his time. He was a native of Bruges, as is learned by Van der Straeten after study of the name in contemporary records there.

The first authentic date which we have relative to his career is July 14, 1541; a docu-

ment shows him as second organist at San
Marco, Venice. This position Buus won by
means of a public contest; he received thirteen
of the sixteen votes cast to decide the choice.
And, as Van der Straeten reminds us, we must
not forget that the Flemish artist found himself facing strangers, "always prejudiced and
frequently hostile, and, in his case, called upon
to judge a robust nature which they were
inherently incapable of appreciating fully."
Even this almost unanimous vote left the
authorities of San Marco still hesitating to
give Buus the position which he had so tri-
umphantly won; the Doge was obliged to
make a personal enactment installing him;
"it was the Willaert situation over again."
Buus made the utmost use of his opportunities, and added notably to the brilliancy of
musical Venice.

Nine years later, in 1550, Buus asked for
leave of absence, which was granted him. The
incident which follows has been recorded in
detail in documents and writings of the time.

After four months of his furlough had elapsed, Buus did not reappear in Venice; days, weeks, and months went by and found him still absent. The esteem which he had won for himself may be judged by the fact that, contrary to all precedent, and much against their stiff pride, the procurators of San Marco sent word to Buus through the ambassador at Vienna, asking his intentions and assuring him that he would be welcomed back in Venice.

"Buus replied courteously but firmly that he would gladly devote himself to the service of so glorious a city as Venice and so renowned a position as that of San Marco, but that he must receive a salary in keeping with this eminence," writes Van der Straeten. "He was urged to reduce his demands, which were for two hundred florins a year, but he replied that he was receiving a florin a day where he was, and could give the ambassador no further reply. The council of San Marco must have found the conditions impossible, for they elected Parabosco, a pupil of Willaert."

We must judge Buus fairly in this matter. Necessity caused him to leave Venice; he had been in financial straits when he was first installed there, and was never able to live on his salary. Whether he lived in a manner too luxurious for the situation, or was the victim of poor management we do not know; but documents amply prove his difficulties. He was welcomed with delight at the Austrian court; Ferdinand I was a discriminating patron of the arts. Vienna proved to be a milieu eminently suited to the talents of Buus, and he remained there as court organist; he appears in the official lists until 1564.

The "Ricercari" are his best known works; they are scored for voices, organ, and other instruments. Extant also are songs to French texts and a book of motets.

THOMAS CRÉQUILLON

THIS COMPOSER has left us works which are distinguished even in a period so rich in excellent productions. Concerning his life we know little. It is supposed that he was born near Ghent; we have the record of his death at Béthune in 1557. He was canon at Namur, at Termonde, and finally at Béthune. In the third volume of Van der Straeten's "Musique aux Pays-Bas" Créquillon is mentioned in documents there quoted as "maître de chapelle to Charles V in Spain." This was about 1544.

Ambros has a high opinion of the work of Créquillon. "He ranks among the truly great of his time. His compositions are notable for strength, euphony, spirituality, and simple impressiveness; his place is assured."

Masses were published by Phalèse and Susato, Psalms by Montanus and Neuber. There are extant also motets and French songs.

JACOB REGNART

JACOB was the most important of five Regnart brothers, according to Eitner; Ambros says four. The family came from Douai, where Jacob was born in 1540. He was tenor and second kapellmeister of the Imperial Chapel at

Vienna; a document of August 1, 1573, mentions a payment of fifteen florins to "Jacob Regnart, tenoriste et maître de musique." This document is in the Imperial Library at Vienna. Our scanty information concerning Regnart is owed mainly to the researches of Köchel and Van der Straeten. It is supposed that the composer went to Prague in imperial service, and died there in 1600. Compositions include Masses, motets, and songs to German texts.

PIERRE DE MANCHICOURT

THIS COMPOSER was born at Béthune, as we learn from the title-page of a collection of his works published at Louvain in 1558; he is called Bethunius. A collection of Masses had already been published in Paris in 1532, "furnished with a royal prerogative of 1531." We may conjecture the approximate period of his life, for we have the definite date of his death, recorded on October 5, 1564. Previous to 1545 Manchicourt was maître de choeur at the Cathedral of Tournai, and it appears that he held this position until 1557. He went from there to Antwerp, and is found in May, 1559, at the head of the Flemish Chapel of Philippe at Madrid.

The compositions of Manchicourt were printed by the leading publishers of Paris, Lyons, Antwerp, Venice, Nuremberg, and Louvain.

GHISELIN DANCKERTS

DANCKERTS was born in Tholen, Zeeland. He was clerk of the diocese of Liège in early life; went to Naples in 1538; and in the same year accepted a position as singer in the Papal Chapel, where he remained for many years.

A great part of his fame rests upon his authorship of a treatise pronouncing judgment in a controversy on the use of modes. The treatise is preserved at Rome; it is written in pure Italian, is courteously phrased, and altogether superior to the writings of Vicentino and Lusitano in this controversy.

We have few of his compositions, but Eitner, Van der Straeten, and others consider
them of great merit; Ambros calls them "stiff
and reactionary." Two motets, two madrigals,
and a canon are preserved in Augsburg collections.

HUBERT WAELRANT

WAELRANT was born at Tongerloo, Brabant,
about 1517. The researches of Georg Becker
of Geneva have given us the known biographical details. Becker doubts the correctness of
the general opinion that Waelrant was a pupil
of Willaert. The first authentic information
places him at Antwerp as singer at Notre
Dame. Some years later he founded at Antwerp a music school where he taught solfège
after the method known as Bocedisation, of
which he was the inventor.

In 1554 Waelrant associated himself with a
printer, Jean de Laet of Antwerp, who was a
skilled typographer, as one may judge by
many examples of his work which survive.

Waelrant died at Antwerp, the scene of his entire active and varied career, in 1595. He was the father of several children, one of whom, Raymond, was organist to the Archbishop at Cologne, and later at St. Jacques, in Antwerp, where he was born.

Becker says that Waelrant left compositions of real merit, and "as editor attached his name to a series of publications of high worth." Waelrant's works were published in his own collections and in those of Phalèse. The best-known compositions were the Psalms; he also left motets, madrigals, and songs.

JACHET DE BERCHEM

THE NAME OF THIS COMPOSER is sometimes written Jacquet, and his surname has been attributed to his birthplace, Berchem, a suburb of Antwerp. The date of his birth was shortly after 1500. We know almost nothing concerning the life of this musician, but we have some excellent works.

DUFAY TO SWEELINCK

In the "Introduttorio" of Cinciarino, 1555, Berchem is mentioned as organist of the Duke of Ferrara. The three books of Capriccios of 1561 are dedicated to this same Duke.

Besides these pieces, there were published Masses, motets, and madrigals.

NOE FAIGNEANT

FAIGNEANT is a composer of the middle sixteenth century, as we know from dates of publication of his works; we have no details of his life, except that he is known to have passed some time in Antwerp.

Phalèse published motets, madrigals, and chansons of Faigneant; Jean de Laet of Antwerp issued motets and madrigals; and in the Maldeghem "Trésor" are two madrigals. The Phalèse publication is dated 1569, that of de Laet 1568.

JOSQUIN BASTON

A NETHERLANDS COMPOSER from the first half of the sixteenth century was Baston; from

1552 he was for a short period in the service of the court at Cracow.

In collections published between 1542 and 1559 at Antwerp, Louvain, and Augsburg are 45 motets and a number of songs. Eitner implies, though he does not state, that Baston may have passed some time in Italy.

JACOB VAN WERT

JACOB VAN WERT (Giaches de Wert, Giaches di Reggio) was born in the Netherlands; Ban (Bannius) states that he was a native of Antwerp, and calls him Weert.

He went as a boy to Italy, where he was in the choir at the chapel of the Marchesa della Padulla. He then entered the service of the Duke of Mantua, where he remained all his life. His death occurred there on May 6, 1596, "at the age of sixty," which places his birth in 1536.

In 1565 Wert visited his homeland, returning to Mantua the following year, at which time he was made maestro di capella. His known works consist of motets, madrigals, and many songs, published by Scotto and Gardano and in collections of Phalèse and Proske, and in manuscript in London, Florence, Verona, and Bologna.

VIII
ORLANDE DE LASSUS

O RLANDE DE LASSUS was born at Mons, Hainault, in 1532; this date is established by an inscription on the portrait by Johan Sadeler painted in 1593, "at the age of sixty-one," and by his epitaph, which shows the agreement of his heirs with this date. This must be considered decisive, although Samuel Quickelberg, who was acquainted with Lassus in Munich in 1565, and who wrote the oldest biographical notice concerning him, places the date at 1530.

Many musical historians have made Lassus the object of special study and research; among these may be mentioned Delmotte, Bäumker,

Declève, Destouches, Mathieu, Mantovani, Sandberger, Van der Straeten, and Van den Borren; the last named has published the most recent as well as the fullest and most exact study of the master and his work.

In common with other biographers of Lassus, Van den Borren attacks the ancient piece of misinformation which makes the renowned artist the son of a counterfeiter; his paragraphs on this matter are conclusive: they do not merely attack the libel; they demolish it. Orlande de Lassus is generally known in Belgium as Roland de Lattre, and the form Lassus is considered as a Latinization. This is an error, based on the statement of the Hainault annalist, Vinchant, according to which statement the master changed his original name of de Lattre to escape the shame of the family disgrace. It is true that a Jehan de Lassus was condemned at Mons for counterfeiting in 1550; but there is no remotest particle of evidence connecting this man with the great musician; the name is very common in

that part of the country. This would seem
enough, but Van den Borren goes on to mention an argument which has escaped others.
The name of the criminal was de Lassus, not
de Lattre; there would be no object in chang-
ing from the latter to the former, from a name
with no odium attached to it to one so bur-
dened! The two names are, besides, utterly
without connection: de Lassus derives from
de-là-dessus; de Lattre from de l'Atre. Thus is
this piece , of mediaeval gossip effectively
countered.

Vinchant tells us that Lassus was born in
the "rue dicte Gerlande" (de la guirlande),
and that he was a choirboy in the Church of
St. Nicolas in the Rue Havré. Quickelberg
relates that the young Orlande commenced his
studies at seven years of age, and was taught
the first principles of music at eight and a
half years.

His voice was so beautiful that he was three
times stolen from the school where he lived
with the other choir-boys. We may recall in

this connection the "frantic search," mentioned by Van der Straeten, which was made in the Netherlands for high voices of good quality by agents of the various princes throughout Europe. On the first two occasions the boy Orlande was recovered by his parents; on the third he consented to follow his abductor into the service of Fernand de Gonzaga, Viceroy of Sicily, who was at that time commanding the forces of Charles V at the siege of St. Dizier. This siege took place between the 8th of July and the 7th of August, 1544, when Orlande was about twelve years old.

After the peace of Crespy in September of that year, which peace cut short a march on Paris, Gonzaga set out to return to his estates in Sicily, taking the boy with him. They arrived in Sicily in November of the following year, being delayed for some reason not known to us.

The transfer of Gonzaga to Milan occurred the next May, and again Orlande went with him. In Milan the boy enjoyed the first quiet

existence which he had known since his ab-
duction. The maestro di capella at Milan was
at that time a Netherlander, Verecore, and
Orlande was placed in his choir. When his
voice changed he was taken to Naples, where
he lived for three years with the Marquis de
la Terza. This nobleman was himself a poet, a
man of distinguished taste and real accom-
plishment in the arts. Naples had already enjoyed the musical influence of Tinctoris and
Diego Ortiz, and the environment was an
excellent one for the young musician.

From Naples Lassus went to Rome; after
six months as guest of the Archbishop Alto-
viti, as Quickelberg relates, he was named
director of the choir at San Giovanni Late-
rano. No documents have come to light relative to this activity. What a contrast was the
environment at Rome to that of Naples!
From princely luxury and worldly gayety
to the quietude of a sanctuary; from villanelles
to Masses. The young Palestrina was becoming
known in Rome for his work as master of

the boys at the Julian Chapel, and his devout
and genial efforts, emphasized by his success,
made a deep impression on Lassus. Palestrina was about twenty-eight years old and
Lassus twenty-one when the latter arrived in
Rome.

After two years in Rome, Lassus was re-
called to the Netherlands by the grave illness
of his parents. The journey was long; he arrived to find them already dead. Some writers
state that the composer then went upon a
journey to England in the company of a noble
Italian amateur, Cesare Brancaccio, whose
acquaintance he probably made at Naples;
Brancaccio had a diplomatic mission to fulfill
in England; there are records concerning its
failure and his deportation to France. It is
far from certain that Lassus made this trip to
England or accompanied Brancaccio to France.
What is certain concerning this period is that
Lassus was settled in Antwerp late in 1554 or
early in 1555. This is fixed by a dedication of
his first book of madrigals, villanelles, etc.,

dated May 13, 1555, when he had been already some months in Antwerp.

The Antwerp of that period was a delightful place of residence for a talented young musician. The musical and artistic life was highly developed, and the city was able to sustain this life, being a center of world commerce. The great firms of every country had offices and representatives there. One of the most important of these was that of Fugger, the banking family of Germany, the richest family of that age. The name of Fugger is encountered in every sort of commercial and cultural history of northern Europe for many years.

Such commercial princes as these have at various times had a strong influence on art development. When they are enlightened and cultivated, and their influence is active in behalf of worthy artists, they are benefactors indeed; when, as sometimes happens, they are merely eager for prominence, desirous of being considered lovers of art yet unable to place their patronage with discrimination, such families can hinder or destroy much that is of value, by the negative process of aiding what is mediocre or worse. For it is as impossible for artistic excellence to thrive surrounded by an encouraged mediocrity as it is impossible for delicate flowers to flourish in a bed where weeds are given careful tendance.

Very fortunately the Fuggers were a family of cultivated artistic amateurs; and there were other families of wealthy and discriminating art-lovers in the Netherlands at that time, several of them in Antwerp. These were happy to welcome with enthusiasm an artist so eminently gifted as Lassus. He remained two years in Antwerp, and they must have been two of the pleasantest years of his life.

The reputation of the young musician was made in these years, and his first published works appeared here and in Venice simultaneously. We have already mentioned the book of madrigals and villanelles; this was published by Tielman Susato in 1555. The same year Gardano placed on sale in Venice the first book of Lassus' five-part madrigals. In the next year appeared the first book of the composer's motets, which were issued by Jean de Laet, afterwards the partner of Waelrant.

Established thus in the midst of powerful friends and admirers, and already known as the composer of varied and interesting works published in far separated countries, it is certain that Lassus had a reputation commensurate with his abilities. Albert V, Duke of Bavaria, learned that Antwerp possessed a musician of this distinction, and was desirous of acquiring his services for the ducal chapel. Orlande was invited to Munich in 1556.

The Bavarian Court Chapel had been established since the fourteenth century; the eminent Swiss musician, Senfl, had been active in its service for a number of years previous to the arrival of Lassus, and the reigning duke had increased the personnel of the chapel. From

the autumn of 1556 we have constant mention
of Lassus in the chapel records and those of
the Bavarian court. These records make plain
the importance of the eminent musician in
his new environment. Not that he was given
a high office at once; on the contrary, he
entered as a simple singer, modestly taking his
place without comment. But his genius made
itself felt from the beginning.

In 1560 the Duke sent him on an important
musical mission to the Netherlands; he was
to engage singers and choirboys for the chapel.
This we learn from a letter of Margaret of
Parma, Regent of the Netherlands. She calls
Lassus "maître de chapelle du Duc de Bavi-
ère." The Bavarian records make no mention
at this time of a change in the status of Lassus; Sandberger believes that the advancement
came to him in 1563. Whatever his title,
however, it is plain that Lassus had in 1560
the confidence and respect of his patron, and
was invested with a very real power in the
chapel.

[137]

The first work of the composer to be published in Germany was issued in Nuremberg in 1562 and was dedicated to the Duke. In October of that year Lassus accompanied the Duke on his journey to the coronation of Maximilian II at Frankfort; they visited Prague, Bamberg, and Wurzburg also.

Van den Borren mentions the preparation in 1563 of a codex which contains the Penitential Psalms of Lassus; the two volumes have each a portrait of Lassus "by the court painter, Hans Muelich." We have already been told by Van Aerde that a codex containing works by de Rore had been prepared for Albert by "Johan Mielich, the court painter"; also Ambros, in the third volume of his history, uses this version of the name. The portrait of Lassus shows, says Van den Borren, "a large forehead, somewhat receding, the hair close-cut, the arch of the eyebrow well defined. The eyes are large, and have a rather vague expression, traducing the strength and finesse of Lassus' intelligence.

The nose, 'd'aspect flaireur' (an untranslatable description, this) seems to prolong the receding line of the forehead. The mouth is sensual; the beard is short and cut in a round. The whole appearance of the artist is unusual rather than attractive."

In 1564 and 1565 occurred the first French publication of an entire volume of Lassus' work, by the firm of LeRoy and Ballard; previously these editors had included single pieces in their collections. In 1562 and 1567 Lassus visited Italy to engage singers and players of instruments. During the latter journey occurred the regrettable incident concerning the Duke of Ferrara; to a courteous dedication of a work by Lassus the Duke responded with so niggardly a recognition that "a diplomatic question was avoided only by his supplementing this in an indirect manner." Lassus remained but a short time in Ferrara and returned to Munich.

In the "Discorsi" of Troiano are found descriptions of the many festivities organized

and conducted by Lassus in 1568 on the occasion of the wedding of the young Duke
William with Renée of Lorraine; in these
descriptions Orlande is praised for his polished
and modest manners. The festivities, remarks
Van den Borren dryly, were of a variety and
were given under conditions calculated to
astonish those who still labor under the
delusion that the sixteenth century was devoted entirely to a capella polyphony. Many
works were performed entirely by instruments,
many by instruments and voices, in addition
to those for voices alone.

We learn that in these festivities Lassus
took part also in a comedy improvised for the
occasion; his rôle was that of Lorenzo Magnifico, and "he appeared on the stage wearing
a mask which at first sight raised a shout
of laughter."

In 1570 Lassus was given a patent of nobility, valid for his descendants as well as for
himself; this was bestowed by Maxmilian II.
In 1571 he made a long-desired journey to

Paris. He was received with honor and acclaim; Charles IX showed him every attention, and the publisher, LeRoy, arranged the introduction of everyone of note in Paris at the time. Orlande "returned to Munich loaded with honors and money."

Many letters of Lassus to the young Duke William about this period show us the humor, gayety, and wit of the composer. These letters are written in "a mosaic of French, Latin, and German, following and interlarding each other with burlesque vivacity, giving them a flavor of frolicsome roguery worthy of a college youth in delirium." This gayety was but one side of the nature of Lassus, however; it was a surface covering a character deeply religious and most sensitive. He was at times melancholy, and always introspective. The Penitential Psalms were composed in a sincere outpouring of belief and feeling.

In 1574 Lassus went again to Italy. Interesting letters tell us of his experiences in the Tyrol, experiences which the traveller of today finds unchanged to a startling degree. Arrived in Rome Lassus was received in audience by Pope Gregory XII, who greatly enjoyed meeting the composer, we are told, and who conferred upon him the honorary title of Chevalier de St. Pierre. This Italian voyage of Lassus was not highly successful; only four singers were engaged, with "a viol-player and some dancers." The Duke was not pleased; the journey had been costly; it was not until some months later that serenity was restored between Lassus and his patron.

Magnificent offers were made to Lassus in 1574 by the King of France. Large sums of money and honorable titles were promised him in an invitation sent through his publisher, LeRoy, who doubtless would have been happy to see the great musician established in Paris. As Lassus had already planned his journey to Italy before receiving this invitation, we know that his voyage was not "a start toward Paris, interrupted by news of the death of the French King." This piece of misinformation has been incorporated as fact into some musical histories; but the full correspondence of Lassus, available now, shows clearly that he returned to Munich before May 5th, and the king did not die until May 30th. Another myth concerning Charles IX is that Lassus composed the Penitential Psalms to assuage the King's remorse for the events of St. Bartholomew's Eve; as we know, these Psalms were written thirteen years before that date, and were for the private use of the Duke of Bavaria.

The letters of Lassus to Duke William are particularly frequent and intimate in the years from 1574 to 1578. These missives speak of little dinners, of gardening, of musical jests, and a thousand other trifles in the lives of friends. In 1579 the composer signed an agreement to remain throughout his life at the Bavarian court. Shortly after this Duke Albert died, leaving gigantic state debts to be immediately faced by his son and successor, the genial, light-hearted William.

The first things to be sacrificed to the pressing necessity of the ducal position were the artistic luxuries of Albert; the chapel was reduced at one blow from 44 members to 22; two years later it was further reduced. The payment of gages to Lassus was faithfully carried out, but the musician found himself hampered in all his plans by the small number of performers; he had long been accustomed to having at his command a body of singers and players without parallel in Europe.

Lassus remained faithfully attached to the Bavarian house. He offered to release his claims to funds which he had received from Albert and re-loaned at interest; William, however, would not hear of his sacrificing this part of his earnings. The entire episode is greatly to the credit of both William and Lassus. The Duke, now weighted with cares of State and overwhelmed with debt, changed from the gay young man who had exchanged sprightly letters with Lassus to a careworn, serious ruler. He became deeply religious, and

Munich grew to be a stronghold of Catholicism. This was well suited to the true nature and feelings of Lassus, as we know; he was the loyal friend of the Jesuits at Munich; their Seminary there has a portrait of him. This is a contrast to the former portrait; here the composer is graver, more dignified, and somewhat melancholy.

Lassus went to Italy for the last time in 1585. He made a pilgrimage to Loreto, and afterward visited Ferrara. This time he was received there with the greatest honor. The court of the art-loving Alfonso II enjoyed one of the earliest and most complete orchestras of Europe; remembering the delight of Lassus in using the instrumental facilities at his disposal in Munich, we may imagine his deep pleasure in the performances at Ferrara.

Returning to Munich Lassus became more and more subject to melancholia. His physician was one of his best friends; the relations with the ducal family were all that could be wished, and Lassus was given every honor and privilege which the Duke was able to bestow; there was no true cause for the gloom which clouded the days of the master. It was disease and not reality which tormented him. He passed from his suffering to death in 1594. His heirs erected a monument the following year; it is now in the Bavarian National Museum. But no monument is needed to Orlande de Lassus. His own work is the most glorious of monuments.

The compositions of Orlande de Lassus may be divided into eight groups: Motets; Masses; Magnificats; Passions; madrigals; villanelles, moresques, and miscellaneous pieces; French songs; German lieder.

The motets form the most important group of his works, both from the point of view of musical value and that of numerical preponderance. The sons of Lassus, Ferdinand and Rodolphe, issued in 1604 a collection as complete as possible, calling it "Magnum opus musicum." This collection contains one hundred motets for four voices, 24 for two voices, 24 for three, 167 for five, 159 for six, 11 for seven, 24 for eight, two for nine, three for ten, and two for twelve voices.

Among the motets must be included the Penitential Psalms, which were composed for Duke Albert, and not published until 1584, five years after the Duke's death. These Psalms are for five voices, but various sections of single numbers are for two, three, or four voices. Also among the motets are: the "Lectiones," in two parts, one with text from Job, and one concerning the Nativity; Offices, five in number; the Stabat Mater; and Lamentations (five voices).

The Magnificats were published complete by Rodolphe de Lassus in 1619. This edition included the Nuremberg collection, those of the Patrocinium of 1576 and of 1587, and sixteen posthumous works.

The Passions are four in number; one was included in the Patrocinium of 1575.

The madrigals of Lassus comprise the sec-

ond, fourth, sixth, eighth, and tenth volumes of the magnificent Breitkopf and Härtel
edition of the complete works, which edition
was begun in 1894 to commemorate the 300th
anniversary of his death. The eighty-nine
madrigals for five voices appeared in a half-
dozen volumes published between 1555 and
1587, and in a series of collections issued at
different dates. There are forty-one four-voice
madrigals; thirteen of these were published
prior to 1560, the rest between that date and
1587. The six-voice pieces were all published
after 1578. There are two madrigals for seven
voices, and three for ten.

The villanelles, songs concerning the loves
of peasants and shepherds, are souvenirs of the
Neapolitan period of Lassus; they are written
principally to texts in the Neapolitan dialect
and are eighteen in number. The moresques
are dialogues, serenades, etc., concerning
Giorgia, Lucia, Cathalina, Zanni, and other
figures; the patois of the Moorish-Italian
lower classes is used for the texts of most of

these pieces. They show an aspect of the composer which reflects his observations of the tumultuous and teeming life of Naples' streets. They are, on occasion, far from edifying.

The French songs number 146; they form the twelfth, fourteenth, and sixteenth volumes of the complete works. There are 67 for four voices, 58 for five, one for three, four for six, and five for eight.

The German lieder are 93 in number; 25 for three voices, 17 for four, 41 for five, nine for six, and one for eight.

IX

JAN PIETERSZOON SWEELINCK

O<small>F THAT PHENOME-</small>
<small>NAL LINE</small> of Netherlands musical geniuses ex-
tending unbroken from the time of Dufay to
his own, Sweelinck was the most important
from the viewpoint of the development of
modern music; he marks the first entry into
music history of an influence preponderantly
instrumental; his example as composer and
his gifts and authority as teacher made possible the work of Bach and the moderns.

Sweelinck was born in Amsterdam in 1562.
His father was Pieter, organist of the Oude
Kerk, a musician of ability and the boy's first
teacher. Pieter Sweelinck died in 1573, but it

is plain that the son must have continued his musical study diligently and with good guidance, for at the age of fifteen he went to Venice and was accepted as a pupil in theory by the great Zarlino, and in organ playing by Andrea Gabrieli.

These musicians were two of the most distinguished disciples of Willaert, the great Netherlander, founder of the Venetian School. The young Giovanni Gabrieli, nephew of Andrea, was but five years older than Sweelinck; he had already begun his brilliant career, having published at eighteen his first book of madrigals. From Hassler we learn of the interest taken in young Sweelinck by all these eminent musicians.

In 1580 Sweelinck returned to Amsterdam, aged eighteen; he was at once given the position formerly held by his father at the Oude Kerk, a position which meanwhile had been passing from one incumbent to another without satisfactory results. The able musicianship of the youth must have been evident to the authorities, since they were willing to overlook his lack of years. From this time until the end of his life Sweelinck worked in Amsterdam, holding the same post in the church, teaching and composing.

Documents of the period show that Sweelinck received only one hundred gulden per year in the early years as organist. Tiedeman, the Dutch writer, remarks that "in his case, the stomach of nineteen would not be too well filied on that fabulous sum." In 1586 the salary was doubled; in 1590 it was increased to three hundred gulden. At his marriage in that same year, Sweelinck was offered the choice between a further yearly amount of one hundred gulden and the free use of a house. He chose the latter, and "moved from the then very unfashionable Kalverstraat to Koestraat." His new home was a house which had been a convent and had come into possession of the city; Sweelinck remained in this dwelling until his death, as the records show.

DUFAY TO SWEELINCK

There is a story, mentioned by several writers, of a purse made up for Sweelinck by a number of wealthy merchants; this sum they handled for his benefit, crediting him with all winnings, and paying losses out of their own pockets. After many years the amount is said to have reached forty thousand gulden. The city purchased in 1604 a "clavicymbel" for his use; and in 1605 "a cloth cover for the same."

We possess two portraits of Sweelinck. One is dated 1606, with the inscription: "Aetatis 44 ao. 1606 M. JO. SWEL. AMS. OR." This portrait shows us a "handsome, manly face, from whose features speak a deep earnestness, but also goodness and kindness." The second portrait is often reproduced; in its inscription the musician is called "Musicus et Organista toto orbe celeberrimus. Vir singulari modestia ac pietate, cum in vita, tum in morte omnibus suspiciendus." It is a woodcut, dated 1624; Plemp wrote the lines on this picture, beginning:

[153]

DUFAY TO SWEELINCK

Joannes Petrus Swelingus Amsterodamus,
Qui fuit organica Pallas in arte minor.
Cujus fama Italos tetigit salsoque Brittanos,
Quique, Orlande, tuis notus erat Bavaris.
Omnibus ex terris peregrinas traxerat Aures—

This portrait appeared three years after the death of Sweelinck, which occurred at Amsterdam on October 16, 1621.

Sweelinck's work as a teacher was of incalculable importance. His fame attracted to him the finest talents among the young organists and composers of the time. Thanks to the researches of the eminent musical historian, Eitner, in Berlin, Hamburg, Königsberg, and Dantzig, we have very full information concerning the magnificent North German organ school of the seventeenth century, whose founders were all devoted pupils of Sweelinck in Amsterdam. The most important of these were Jacob Praetorius and Heinrich Scheidemann of Hamburg, Samuel Scheidt of Halle, Paul Seifert of Dantzig, and Melchior Schildt of Hanover.

This group, gifted, famous, and widely influential, is an extraordinary one to emanate from the teaching of one man. A document from Breslau, found by Eitner, contains the following passage: "Jacob Praetorius (Schultz), son of Hieronymus, was born about 1600 in Hamburg; he trod in the steps of his distinguished father, and became organist of the Jacobikirche. He wished, however, to perfect himself further, so was given by the authorities of the church a leave of two years, with full consent to betake himself to Amsterdam, there to study with the 'organist-maker,' Sweelinck. With him went Heinrich Scheidemann."

Scheidemann was organist of the Katharinenkirche in Hamburg, and was the teacher of Reinken, one of the greatest of the seventeenth century musicians. Reinken was born in 1621 at Deventer, Holland, but came early to Hamburg; there he exerted a powerful influence as organist, composer, and teacher. In one of his famous theoretical works Reinken speaks of "the unequalled master, Jan Pieters-zoon Sweelinck, upon whose rules of composition this work is based." Reinken was the founder of the "Hamburg School" of organ-playing, composition, and theory. We have records of the many occasions on which Bach walked to Hamburg to hear the playing of Reinken; it is now the opinion of many authorities that Bach availed himself of these opportunities to study with the man whom he so deeply revered. At any rate, he was influenced in every musical activity of his later life by Reinken, and was thus a direct product of the artistic principles of Sweelinck.

From Johann Heintzsch we have a tribute to the master as a teacher: "Sweelinck was considered 'a wonder of music.' When the fame of his greatness went abroad, the young talent of Germany flocked to him, and Hamburg called him 'the organist-maker.' The two Hamburg masters, Praetorius and Scheidemann, honored him as a father. They learned from him not only music, but also principles of conduct, and brought away from their association with him a lifelong ideal, which they kept ever before their eyes, and which they set before their famous pupils."

The best-known among Sweelinck's Dutch pupils was Dr. Cornelis Gijsbertszoon, who is better known as Plemp, a poet and Latin scholar as well as a gifted musical amateur. His relations with Sweelinck were not only those of teacher and pupil but also of two very dear friends. Plemp was a man of excellent social position, a friend of the famous Hooft family.

The intercourse between Sweelinck and his pupils seems to have been friendly and hearty, and it lasted after they returned to their distant homes. Scheidt joined with Sweelinck in the editing of some songs; Sweelinck prepared a "Canticum" in celebration of the marriage of Praetorius; he wrote a canon in honor of Scheidemann, with this dedication: "Ter eeren des vromen Jongkmans Henderich Scheydman van Hamborgh, is dit geschreven bij mij, Jan P. Sweelinck, organist tot Amsterdam, op den 12den Novemb., 1614." For the cantor, Johann Stobaeus, of Königsberg, Sweelinck wrote another "Canticum" in 1617.

The fame of Sweelinck in his own land was very great, but the records concerning his pupils are not so full as those of Germany. A document from Rotterdam mentions the fact that the city paid its organist a sum of money "with which to go to Amsterdam and learn to improve his playing by study with Jan P. Sweelinck." Sweertius, Dr. Wassenaer, and the poet Vondel are among the Dutch writers who pay glowing tribute to Sweelinck.

The influence of Sweelinck, so powerful in Germany and the Netherlands, we find active also in England and in Italy. The instrumental compositions of Sweelinck were highly considered in England. Some of them are to be found in the virginal book of Queen Elizabeth, who was an excellent amateur. The famous virtuoso and composer, John Bull, seems to have been in close artistic relation with Sweelinck.

Dr. Bull was engaged from 1613 as organist at Brussels, and Max Seiffert assumes that he visited Amsterdam. "Their mutual esteem is striking," he says. Sweelinck included one of Bull's canons in his work on counterpoint, and the English musician composed a fantasie upon a theme of his colleague's.

One of the musicians of greatest importance to Italy at this period was the young Girolamo Frescobaldi. He travelled to the Netherlands, where Sweelinck was already a mature and famous artist. Frescobaldi used the principles of Sweelinck in his works, and his pupil, Froberger, composed a Toccata upon a theme of Sweelinck's. Frescobaldi and Froberger gave immense impetus and prestige to the methods and principles of Sweelinck, not only in Italy but also in South Germany, where their renown was great. Long before this we find, however, that Sweelinck was a powerful influence in South Germany; Christian Erbach of Augsburg wrote a "Canzone cromatica" in which Sweelinck's distinctive chromatic sequences are used. We find in the Canzone of Bach (Peters IV, 10) these typical Sweelinck devices, as Seiffert and others have noted.

Max Seiffert, editor of Sweelinck's works, has written an accurate and painstaking biographical sketch of the composer. Previously F. H. L. Tiedeman had written one, based on long study of Dutch archives. Robert Eitner made exhaustive research in Germany, as well as informing himself thoroughly on all Dutch records; he wrote a remarkable biography which has remained in manuscript. These three eminent historians agree on the main facts of Sweelinck's career.

One of the most important among these facts is, of course, the Venetian study of Sweelinck. Among the bases for the concurring judgments of Seiffert, Tiedeman, and Eitner on this matter is the aforementioned record by Hans Leo Hassler, direct from Venice. After most careful study of the three biographies, and many of the original sources of the works, the writer also is convinced that the matter is beyond dispute.

Eitner sums up, beautifully and profoundly, the importance of Sweelinck in music development; I quote from his manuscript biography in Amsterdam:

"How marvellously entwined are the threads of intellectual power! They join the apparently distant Zarlino in Italy with the young Sweelinck, by whom the highest achievements of contrapuntal art are brought from Venice to northern Europe.

"Again: the old art is in danger of degenerating; few uphold its glorious traditions. In Hamburg works Reinken, a fiery adherent of Sweelinck. Like a rock he stands against the musical trifling of the time, waiting for someone worthy to inherit his traditions and his skill. At last, out of Saxony, there comes to him the young Sebastian Bach. Joyfully recognizing this lofty spirit, Reinken makes him his heir. The old art soars again to new and untried heights."

The complete known works of Sweelinck
were edited for the Vereeniging voor Noord-
Nederland's Muziekgeschiedenis by Prof. Dr.
Max Seiffert, and published by Breitkopf and
Härtel and Martinus Nijhoff between 1895 and
1903. They comprise, in the Dutch edition,
ten volumes, divided as follows:

I.

Works for organ and clavichord

II.

First book of Psalms (4, 5, 6, and 7 voices)

III.

Second book of Psalms (4, 5, 6, 7, and 8
voices)

IV.

Third book of Psalms (the same)

V.

Fourth book of Psalms (the same)

VI.

Cantiones sacrae (5 voices)

VII.

Chansons (5 voices, French text)

VIII.

Rimes françoises et italiennes (2, 3, and one
for 4 voices)

IX.

Occasional Compositions: Ricercar, Pavane
with variations for clavichord, canons, the
Canticum for Praetorius, the Canticum for
Stobaeus, etc.

X.

Rules for Composition (edited by Dr. H. Gehr-
mann, German text only)

INDEX

Italics indicate principal reference

[165]

INDEX

Dufay, Guillaume, 14, *18*, 21, 26, 31, 150

E

Eitner, Robert, 19, 23, 25, 28, 40, 44, 56, 62, 63, 64, 69, 71, 89, 97, 109, 111, 120, 123, 126, 154, 155, 160, 161
Elizabeth, Queen of England, 158
Eloy, 28
Erasmus, Desiderius (Geert), 36, 38, 44
Erbach, Christian, 159
Este, Hercules (Ercole) I, d', Duke of Ferrara, 45, 50
Este, Hercules (Ercole) IV, d', Duke of Ferrara, 99
Expert, Henri, 58, 61

F

Faigneant, Noë, 125
Faugues, Vincent, 26
Ferdinand of Aragon, King of Naples, 70
Ferdinand I, Emperor, 119
Fétis, François, 29, 39, 62, 79, 88, 108
Fevin, Antoine, 67
Finck, Hermann, 18, 21, 88, 108
First Netherlands School, 13
Florio, Francesco, 33
Forkel, Johann Nikolas, 19
Francis I of France, 65
Frescobaldi, Girolamo, 159
Froberger, Johann, 159
Fugger, Jean-Jacques, 134

G

Gabrieli, Andrea, 74, 76, 78, 151
Gabrieli, Giovanni, 76, 77, 151
Gafor (Gaforio), Franchino, 18, 21, 29, 65
Gardano (Gardane), Antonio, 81, 101, 102, 116, 127, 136
Gaspar (van Weerbeke), 42, *63*

Ghizegem, Heinrich van, see Heyne
Gijsbertszoon, Cornelis, 153, 157
Glarean (Loris), Heinrich, 39, 44, 50, 65, 66, 67, 68
Gombert, Nicolas, *103*, 114
Gonzaga, Fernand de, 131
Grégoir, Edouard Georges, 74, 75, 79
Gregory XII, Pope, 142
Gritti, Andrea, Doge of Venice, 80

H

Haberl, Franz Xaver, 19, 28, 71
Hassler, Hans Leo von, 151, 160
Hawkins, Sir John, 18, 87
Henry VIII of England, 112
Heyden, Seybald, 18
Heyne, 24

J

Jacotin (Jacques Godebrye), 69
Jacotino, 69
Jannequin, Clément, 113
Josquin, see Deprès

K

Kiesewetter, Raphael Georg, 19, 37, 62
Köchel, Ludwig von, 88, 121

L

Laet, Jean de, 123, 125, 136
Landino, Francesco, 78
La Rue, Pierre de, 37, 40, *56*
Lassus, Orlande de, 82, 100, *128*, 154
Lassus, Ferdinand de, 146
Lassus, Rodolphe de, 146
Le Maistre, Mattheus, 112
Le Roy, Adrien, 81, 96, 101, 139, 141, 142
Lorenzo Magnifico, see Medici
Louis XI of France, 33, 36
Louis XII of France, 50, 65, 74
Loyset, see Compère
Ludwig, King of Hungary, 75

INDEX

INDEX